CW00666574

Sep–Dec 2024

Day by Day
with
God

Rooting women's lives in the Bible

BRF
Ministries

 Ministries

15 The Chambers, Vineyard
Abingdon OX14 3FE
+44 (0)1865 319700 | brf.org.uk

Bible Reading Fellowship is a charity (233280)
and company limited by guarantee (301324),
registered in England and Wales

ISBN 978 1 80039 264 9

This edition © 2024 Bible Reading Fellowship
Cover image © Cavan Images / Alamy Stock Photo
Photos of the editor and contributors are used with kind permission

Distributed in Australia by:
MediaCom Education Inc, PO Box 610, Unley, SA 5061
Tel: 1 800 811 311 | admin@mediacom.org.au

Distributed in New Zealand by:
Scripture Union Wholesale, PO Box 760, Wellington
Tel: 04 385 0421 | suwholesale@clear.net.nz

Acknowledgements
Scripture quotations marked with the following abbreviations are taken from the version
shown. Where no abbreviation is given, the quotation is taken from the same version as
the headline reference. NIV: The Holy Bible, New International Version (Anglicised edition)
copyright © 1979, 1984, 2011 by Biblica. Used by permission of Hodder & Stoughton
Publishers, a Hachette UK company. All rights reserved. 'NIV' is a registered trademark of
Biblica. UK trademark number 1448790. NKJV: The New King James Version®. Copyright ©
1982 by Thomas Nelson. Used by permission. All rights reserved. MSG: *The Message*, copyright
© 1993, 1994, 1995, 1996, 2000, 2001, 2002 by Eugene H. Peterson. Used by permission
of NavPress. All rights reserved. Represented by Tyndale House Publishers, Inc. TPT: The
Passion Translation®. Copyright © 2017, 2018, 2020 by Passion & Fire Ministries, Inc. Used
by permission. All rights reserved. thePassionTranslation.com. ESV: The Holy Bible, English
Standard Version, published by HarperCollins Publishers, © 2001 Crossway Bibles, a division
of Good News Publishers. Used by permission. All rights reserved. NLT: The Holy Bible, New
Living Translation, copyright © 1996, 2004, 2007, 2013. Used by permission of Tyndale House
Publishers, Inc., Carol Stream, Illinois 60188. All rights reserved. AMP: The Amplified® Bible
(AMP), Copyright © 2015 by The Lockman Foundation. Used by permission.
www.Lockman.org. NCV: The New Century Version®. Copyright © 2005 by Thomas Nelson.
Used by permission. All rights reserved.

A catalogue record for this book is available from the British Library

Printed and bound in the UK by Zenith Media NP4 0DQ

Day by Day with God

with

Edited by **Jackie Harris**　　　September–December 2024

Writers in this issue

Jen Baker is a speaker, author and mentor. Her mission is to see a global movement of Christian women living with courageous faith and creating kingdom impact.

Hannah Fytche is studying for her PhD in theology at the University of Cambridge. She has been writing for BRF Ministries since 2015, when she wrote her first book, *God's Daughters*, and has written for *Day by Day with God* since 2018.

Anne Le Tissier is an author, preacher and conference speaker, called to disciple others in their ongoing walk with God. She has been writing for *Day by Day with God* since 2005. Connect with her at **anneletissier.com**.

Christine Platt has lived and ministered in the UK, Africa and Asia. She has written several Bible study booklets and devotional notes in multiple languages. She currently lives in New Zealand and teaches English to Asian immigrants.

Amy Boucher Pye is a London-based writer, speaker, retreat leader and spiritual director. She's the author of several books and has an MA in Christian spirituality from the University of London. Find her at **amyboucherpye.com**.

Tracy Williamson lives in Kent, working with blind singer/songwriter Marilyn Baker for MBM Trust. Her latest book is *Unashamed: Discover the healing power of God's love for your wounded soul* (Authentic Media, 2023). Connect with her at **mbm-ministries.org**.

Rachel Turner is the discipleship pastor at Hope Church, Harrogate and the founder of Parenting for Faith. She is an international speaker and author of ten books, including *Parenting Children for a Life of Faith*, *It Takes a Church to Raise a Parent* and *Comfort in the Darkness*.

Emma Scrivener was born in Belfast, but now lives with her husband and two children in southeast England. She is the author of several books, including *A New Name* and *A New Day* (IVP), and blogs at **emmascrivener.net**.

Sheila Jacobs is a writer, an editor and an award-winning author. She lives in rural north Essex, attends an Elim church where she serves as deacon and is a day chaplain at a retreat centre.

Michele D. Morrison is a freelance writer, wife, mother and grandmother. She loves digging into God's word, listening for God's voice in the daily routines of life and blogging at **tearsamidthealiencorn.blogspot.com**.

Welcome

Someone once described reading Bible notes as like hanging out with a group of friends who you chat things over with. We love to think that *Day by Day with God* feels like that. We may not always agree, and there may be some individuals we feel more or less comfortable with, but overall we feel better for having spent time together and appreciate that we are all seeking to grow in our relationship with God and understanding of his word.

If you are a regular reader of these notes, you will recognise most of our contributors, but we are pleased to welcome Emma Scrivener and Jen Baker to the team. Both are authors and speakers; Emma grew up in Belfast but now lives in the south of England, and Jen grew up in the USA before moving to the UK in 2003.

With her deep love for the Bible and a passion to see lives changed, Jen starts us off with a study of James. She says studying James is like being on a beautiful journey, and we hope that will be your experience as you work through the topics in this issue.

We'll be tackling some familiar passages – the parable Jesus told of the prodigal son and the Christmas story – but we'll be seeking fresh interpretations and asking questions of these well-known passages. We'll be learning from the lives of Solomon and John the Baptist, and working through the book of Joel.

For those who like a topical study, we'll discover what the Bible says about family and the different family structures we find within its pages, and we consider what the Bible says about home and how often homes play a key part in biblical stories.

We'll also be encouraged to consider what is needed to enjoy a deeper intimacy with God and seek refreshment and inspiration from the Psalms.

Augustine of Hippo wrote: 'The holy scriptures are our letters from home.' Let's read them together and pray for each other, that we will hear what God wants to say to us, remind us of or call us to do.

Teach us, Father God, as we reflect on your words. May we hear your voice through the stories of long ago guiding us, comforting us, challenging us where necessary and reminding us of where we belong. Amen.

Jackie Harris, Editor

James: journey into life

Jen Baker writes:

The book of James should come with a label that says: 'Warning, this book is not for the fainthearted and will likely cause some distress!' The themes and topics it covers can be applied to nearly every area of our lives, regardless of our age or circumstances. James' writing contains several hard-hitting truths which have the potential to unlock our file drawer of excuses and tamper with any well-established comfort zones. To put it bluntly, after reading this book we cannot say, 'I don't know how to live the Christian life.'

Please don't let the warning label put you off, though! The truths in this book are seeds of gold waiting to produce a harvest of freedom. Words, works and wisdom are repetitive themes throughout the book; they are not always obvious but the underlying truths of watching our words, honouring God through our works and being led by wisdom are repeatedly woven throughout the chapters.

Over the next two weeks we will cover the whole book of James in our daily readings. I would encourage you to view each reading through the lenses of words, works and wisdom, deciding each day where your perspective might need tweaking, if not cleansing.

In my group mentoring, I repeatedly say, 'We don't do shame and we don't do guilt', because our Heavenly Father does not have any part of these vices; they are always found in the enemy's tool belt. We are under grace (Romans 6:14), and it would benefit us to read the book of James from that position. If we aim for perfection, we will easily become depressed, frustrated and achievement-focused, which is the opposite of what James is teaching us. Our transformative journey is ongoing until we meet Jesus face-to-face and are fully conformed into his likeness (2 Corinthians 3:18). What a glorious day that will be!

Therefore, might I suggest instead of perfection we aim for partnership? As you read, I want you to imagine Jesus sitting with you and cheering you on; the Heavenly Father loving you while you wrestle with hidden places in your heart; and the Holy Spirit counselling you as you unpick deep truths found in scripture.

On second thought, perhaps the warning label should read: 'Warning, beautiful journey ahead.'

Count it all joy

Consider it pure joy, my brothers and sisters, whenever you face trials of many kinds. (v. 2, NIV)

If there was a vote on which sentence we wanted deleted from the Bible, I'm pretty certain verse two of this first chapter would make the top ten. How many of us, after reading the verse, have wanted to text James with an emoji-laden 'Are you kidding me?'

I've imagined him penning those words after emerging from a great time of worship which had caused his trials to be clouded by the afterglow of God's presence. Surely the challenges he faced weren't nearly as daunting as those we're battling in our lives today. Then I remember he was one of the early pillars in the church community (Acts 15:13) and historically is thought to have been martyred by being stoned to death. Okay, maybe he does speak with some authority.

Joy can be found in the harshest of seasons. James says we should consider it 'pure joy', and to consider means to think carefully about something or to ponder on it. It is intentional. Therefore, when trials come, we have a choice: deliberately tap into our joy or be led by our feelings.

I didn't become a Christian until I was 19 and up to that point feelings ruled my life. It never occurred to me that God had given us something – the fruit of the Spirit, which includes joy (Galatians 5:22–23) – that could override our feelings, regardless of our external circumstances.

After enduring painful trials and making a few feeble attempts to let God's word win over my whinging, I began noticing that out of the fire I was emerging stronger, bolder and wiser. The more I pressed into praise and trust, the less I felt confusion and fear. Perhaps James is on to something after all?

Lord, thank you for the joy and peace we have been given by the Holy Spirit living within us. I hand you my worries and cares, knowing they are safer in your hands than in my heart. Amen.

JEN BAKER

Wisdom over worry

Such a person is double-minded and unstable in all they do. (v. 8, NIV)

Have you ever stood in front of the open refrigerator bemoaning the fact there is nothing to eat as you stare at enough food to feed a small village? Can anyone relate to choosing prudence over preference when out to dinner with friends, resulting in food envy after the food arrives?

Indecision and regret have stolen hours (lifetimes) from too many people over the years, and I knew that it was regularly stealing mine. I grew up with tremendous insecurity, never wanting to put myself forward in case I looked foolish or, even worse, found myself standing alone. This fear of other people's opinions caused me to vacillate over the simplest of decisions, wasting hours of my life that I can never get back.

It wasn't until I was an adult well into my 40s that I decided I would no longer be a victim to indecision. I started audibly declaring, 'I am proactive and quick to make good decisions' each morning as I was getting ready. That one statement literally began changing my life. If I was indecisive at the refrigerator, I would repeat my declaration and then force myself to make a quick decision. When I was dining out with friends, I inwardly challenged myself to be the first person who chose her meal. Making life decisions became faster as I trusted my gut and believed that even if I got it wrong God would make it right.

If you find yourself in a place of instability or confusion, pause and ask for wisdom, then proactively follow whichever choice brings a calm to your inner being. Just as double-mindedness causes instability, single-mindedness can bring sure footedness when it is led by God's perfect peace.

If you struggle with indecision, begin declaring to yourself that you are single-minded and stable in all your ways. Don't go by what you see but trust God's Spirit to bring the stability for which you have been created.

JEN BAKER

What do you hear?

My dear brothers and sisters, take note of this: Everyone should be quick to listen, slow to speak and slow to become angry. (v. 19, NIV)

Imagine a world where people stop to listen before they speak. What a different world we would be experiencing!

Instead of jumping to conclusions and shouting at the careless driver, letting the waitress know the service has been slow or judging the doctor for the length of time test results have taken, maybe we should consider what the other person is facing? Could it be that the driver has just been bereaved, the waitress is about to be evicted or the doctor hasn't slept in 24 hours?

I have to regularly remind myself that everyone is facing a challenge: the businesswoman you pass on the street, the person who serves you at the till, the child throwing a tantrum or the unengaged spouse all battle some type of uncertainty, fear, hope deferred, confusion or a multitude of other trials that happen because we live in a fallen world.

James asks us to look beyond ourselves to the needs of others and reminds us that we should not only study scripture, but also respond to what it teaches us. We can do this by speaking in love, sharing with others, visiting orphans and widows and being a godly representation of Jesus Christ.

Imagine Jesus interrupting someone who was talking, erupting in anger when his food wasn't ready on time or giving the cold shoulder to a disciple who had been acting less than godly that day. It's unthinkable!

I believe one key to Jesus' compassion is his ability to listen. Let's begin listening to the story, the pain, the confusion and the history of the one who is hurting us. It doesn't justify bad behaviour, but it can soften our hurting heart. As we read elsewhere in scripture, 'A soft answer turns away wrath' (Proverbs 15:1, NKJV).

If someone has hurt you and you are struggling to forgive them, ask the Holy Spirit to show you his heart for that person. Then pray as you are able, asking God to bless them and lead them into freedom.

JEN BAKER

Mercy or judgement?

Talk and act like a person expecting to be judged by the Rule that sets us free. For if you refuse to act kindly, you can hardly expect to be treated kindly. Kind mercy wins over harsh judgement every time. (vv. 12–13, MSG)

All of us deserve punishment for having sinned and fallen short of the glory of God (Romans 3:23). Yet, because of Christ taking our place, dying on the cross and destroying the power of death, our punishment has been removed and replaced by a glorious mercy that we do not deserve. Thank you, Jesus!

It's helpful to remember that God's justice is not the opposite of God's mercy but rather God's mercy is revealed through God's justice. In other words, he loved us enough to send his only Son to take our punishment so that justice could be satisfied; that is mercy.

James does not mince his words here. He clearly says that by refusing kindness, which is walking in judgement, we are reverting to a lifestyle of legalism. Ouch. Let's apply this concept of justice and mercy to those we may strongly disagree with, including politicians, and people on social media, on television or in the streets.

How easy it is to judge them and forget the grace under which we live every moment of our day! When I treat someone as less than, I'm inferring I am more than. If I'm not careful that pride will lead me on to a judgement seat not meant for me. Am I all knowing? Have I walked in their shoes? Were they given the same set of blessings and equipping I have experienced in my life?

There is often a fine line between judgement and discernment, and a wise woman will tread this line carefully. While we cannot judge a person's heart, we are asked to judge their fruit, and it is there that the body of Christ must use discernment – discernment led by kindness, not criticism.

Lord, I understand judgement comes from a critical spirit, so please give me a heart of compassion for those I am tempted to judge. I want to see others through your eyes of love and not my eyes of pride. Amen.

JEN BAKER

Living as God's friend

You see that his faith and his actions were working together, and his faith was made complete by what he did. And the scripture was fulfilled that says, 'Abraham believed God, and it was credited to him as righteousness,' and he was called God's friend. (vv. 22–23, NIV)

Best friends are those who stick with us through thick and thin. They don't leave when life gets tough or uncomfortable, but they go the extra mile to resolve conflict and walk in love. How would you describe your friendship with God? Does it shift with changing seasons or remain steadfast regardless of your circumstances?

In this passage Abraham is called a friend of God during the worst season of his life, when he was asked to sacrifice his much-loved son. Was it his faith that developed this friendship or the friendship which developed his faith?

In 2 Chronicles 20, we see that Abraham's friendship left a legacy still called upon by kings long after he had passed away. Jehoshaphat, king of Judah, was being attacked by the enemy when he reminded God of his friendship with Abraham and his promise to keep all of Abraham's descendants safe (vv. 7–9), a promise that extends to our lives today (Galatians 3:29).

Regardless of our position as a (spiritual) descendent of Abraham, a faith not tested remains only theory and never legacy. Yet, if Abraham's friendship with God helped establish a legacy of faith, wouldn't it make sense that our intimacy also carries the potential to surpass personal benefit, leaving in its wake a legacy seen by future generations?

Faith was completed by works – works between two friends (Abraham and God) who trusted one another to bring heaven's plans to fruition on earth. Today let's spend time with a friend who has taken our place in death and opened up the road to life, a friend who sticks closer than a brother, loves deeper than a mother and remains closer than any other: Jesus.

Lord, forgive me for making my friendship with you one-sided at times. I want to trust you even when I don't understand, because deep down, I know that you are good. Please help me in this journey. Amen.

JEN BAKER

Taming the tongue

Out of the same mouth come praise and cursing. My brothers and sisters, this should not be. Can both fresh water and salt water flow from the same spring? (vv. 10–11, NIV)

While the book of James is known for numerous hard-hitting truths, I believe the verses about our tongue are some of the most well-known and most challenging. Earlier in the chapter, James says that if anyone tames their tongue, they will be perfect (v. 2), but then he expounds the impossibility of that task. He doesn't mince words when he says, 'The tongue also is a fire' (v. 6) and 'No human being can tame the tongue. It is a restless evil, full of deadly poison' (v. 8).

We have all experienced times when regrettable words flew out of our mouths faster than the hallelujahs at a camp meeting. Our words may have lasted a moment, but the memory left behind can last a lifetime. I remember a time when the Lord highlighted the sheer depravity of what was coming out of my mouth, spotlighting the pain residing in my heart. I was a pastor at the time and, without realising it, I had learned the art of covering up with those I led and letting loose to those I loved.

In Luke 6:45 it says that out of the overflow of the heart the mouth speaks; what is inside can be seen outside. Realising that I couldn't blame my poor behaviour on stress, spiritual warfare or mood swings was a painful journey. I had chosen to treat others as less significant than myself, and it was sin. Once I owned up to my words, the Spirit of God began cleaning up my heart.

Let today be a day of cleansing, repenting and choosing to see the incredible responsibility of owning a muscle which, when used correctly, can bring blessing, joy, peace and transformation to a hurting world.

If you are bold enough, ask someone close to you what your words reveal about your heart. Are they life-filled, fear-filled, hope-filled or…? Take that answer to the Lord and listen for his guidance.

JEN BAKER

Sowing in peace

For where you have envy and selfish ambition, there you find disorder and every evil practice. (v. 16, NIV)

This verse has convicted me more times than I can count! I knew if anyone looked into my heart, they would see envy and selfish ambition enthusiastically waving back at them like a three-year old at the Christmas nativity who waves to her parents. It wasn't that I wanted to be centre stage; I was much too insecure for that. No, I opened the door to envy and ambition because I wanted to assist God with his plans for my life. Initially my desire was innocent, but I have learned that unchecked desire can become unwanted bondage.

We're about halfway through the book of James, and it's here that we face another stark reality check as he assures us that our conduct will one day reveal our character. He explains that those who are walking in jealousy and selfishness are being fuelled by the demonic (no mincing words here) and those walking in peace are led by wisdom that comes from heaven. Once again, he presents us with a choice as to which harvest we want to reap: disorder or unity.

One of the clearest examples of this can be seen through the lives of Saul and David in the Old Testament (1 Samuel 16—31). Saul was fuelled by insecurity, jealousy and envy, which eventually stole both his kingship and his life. David, on the other hand, was led by peace, unity and honour, which gave him grace to respond with wisdom and wait on God's timing.

If you find yourself trying to arrange circumstances to open doors, bring 'divine' appointments or make your voice heard, then it would be wise to throw up the white flag of surrender and meditate on these verses until the Holy Spirit saturates you with a peace that goes beyond performance.

Lord, thank you for always working behind the scenes on our behalf. Today I choose to stay in peace as I trust your handiwork of love and wisdom to work all things together for good. Amen.

JEN BAKER

Friendship with the world

You adulterous people, don't you know that friendship with the world means enmity against God? Therefore, anyone who chooses to be a friend of the world becomes an enemy of God. (v. 4, NIV)

How would you define avoiding friendship with the world? Does it mean avoiding television, news reports or friendships with those outside of our faith? A cursory reading of the New Testament, let alone common sense, would disagree with that reasoning. The Oxford English Dictionary defines a friend as: 'A person with whom one has developed a close and informal relationship of mutual trust and intimacy.' Therefore, the question to ask is whether we put more trust in the world than in God's word? Do we feel more comfortable with political correctness or personal holiness?

I think we would agree that in the past ten years (at least) the world has become a darker and more evil place. I have stopped saying that I can't be surprised because I continue to be shocked. Who could have envisioned the danger of gun violence, bullying on social media as well as in the classroom and wondering if what we are seeing is reality or a form of expertly enhanced artificial intelligence?

Friendship starts with a greeting and deepens over time; the same applies to the world. When we assert the opinions and thoughts of the media over God's message, we create a divide only grace can bridge. The other extreme is to close ourselves off, living a super-spiritual existence which refuses to acknowledge deeply rooted pain behind the shallow pleasures so blatantly flaunted in our world today.

How do we avoid the extremes? Jesus said: 'My prayer is not that you take them out of the world but that you protect them from the evil one' (John 17:15). Avoiding friendship with the world is not found in our absence from it but through our protection in it.

Are you putting more focus on people's opinions and society's acceptance rather than on what God has said in his word? If so, consider what might have to change to enable you to love the world but live according to God's ways.

JEN BAKER

Are you fighting or resisting?

Submit yourselves, then, to God. Resist the devil, and he will flee from you. (v. 7, NIV)

My Christian experience seems to include a few good victories overshadowed by years of enemy battle. Can anyone else relate to this? I have personally felt the frustration of repeatedly hearing breakthrough testimonies and 'mountain top' experiences while I (barely) stand there sporting a crooked helmet, holding a well-worn sword, displaying spiritual armour pitted with more holes than a village road after the winter. I wonder when the fighting will stop and when *my* victory will come?

One day as I was reading this passage in James, I realised that the Bible doesn't say fight – it says resist.

Resisting is not the same as fighting. When I resist, I take a stand. I don't allow myself to be pushed and I create barriers to the outside forces attempting to take the ground which I am defending. Fighting carries an implication that the outcome of the battle is yet undecided. Granted, in some Bible passages it talks about fighting (e.g. Ephesians 6:12), but more often we find scriptures that talk about using our authority and walking in the power that we already carry, due to Christ's death on the cross and our inheritance as children of God (Luke 10:19; Matthew 10:1; Daniel 11:32; Zechariah 4:6; Acts 1:8 and many more).

This verse in James reveals that our key to resistance comes from submission. As we submit to our loving Heavenly Father, we are reminded that the battle is not one we have to fight (1 Samuel 17:47; 2 Chronicles 20:15; Psalm 24:8) but one we join with heaven to win. This perspective changes everything! Now we can read the verse with anticipation, knowing the enemy we resist must flee as we stand in faith long enough to see the mountain become our miracle.

Lord, help me see my challenges through the lens of your victory and not the pain of my struggle. Thank you that I never fight alone, but you are always with me in the battle. Amen.

JEN BAKER

Silence the slander

Brothers and sisters, do not slander one another. (v. 11, NIV)

As a child growing up with an older sister, I relished the days she got in trouble while I watched as the 'innocent' bystander. Being a drama queen from a young age, I must admit that I often embellished her actions (apologies to my sister) to whitewash the stain of my own bad behaviour.

We see this replicated around the world today in politics, entertainment, relationships and, sadly, even the church. We might excuse such behaviour in children, but when adults are gossiping, lying or sharing shameful facts about another person it only highlights the jealousy and insecurity in their own hearts.

The book of James reveals this is not just a 21st-century issue. James felt compelled by the Spirit to remind the early church that their words carried judgement they were not empowered to enforce. He set the stage for this concept in our reading yesterday (James 4:6), where he explained humility lays the groundwork for God to be judge and jury, not us.

Who triggers the worst in your words? Where do you find yourself scurrying up the seat of self-righteousness as you look down on one seemingly less perfect? The question at the end of verse 12 – 'Who are you to judge your neighbour?' – is like having a mirror held up in front of us. While it is a rhetorical question, I would suggest our best response is silence before speaking!

Who are we to judge? We who have been forgiven of our own sin, rebellion, lying, cursing and much more. It was our sin that put Christ on the cross, and only from forgiveness can we stand and declare, 'But for the grace of God go I.' The next time we want to judge another person, let's remember that we aren't faultless, simply forgiven.

Take time to search your heart for words spoken in secret or out loud that have torn down instead of built up. Then receive the forgiveness of heaven as you determine to leave judgement to God.

JEN BAKER

Boasting about tomorrow

Why, you do not even know what will happen tomorrow. What is your life? You are a mist that appears for a little while and then vanishes. (v. 14, NIV)

I will never forget visiting New York less than two months after 9/11 and the bombing of the World Trade Center. I was co-leading a group of 70 teenagers and our visit to Ground Zero required an exit off the metro several blocks away from the destruction site. Block after city block, we silently walked the streets, surrounded by people whispering in hushed tones as one would at a funeral. The putrid smell of sulphuric smoke caused us to cover our noses and mouths while we wandered past dust covered shops with their merchandise stolen, broken or destroyed.

Those of an earlier generation may remember the day John F. Kennedy was shot or where they were when the war ended in May 1945. For me, as an American, the 9/11 attacks will forever be a reminder of the day America, and in many respects the rest of the world, changed forever.

All of us have had those unexpected days when the phone rings with heart wrenching news or we have simply been in the wrong place at the wrong time, often left questioning where God was in that moment of shock and pain. Living with mystery is one of the requirements for a child of God. Yet, as our trust in the Lord deepens, our need for answers weakens.

These verses exalt right living over estate planning – an unpopular opinion in society today. Perhaps this is why James could talk about living for today and not boasting about tomorrow; he fully trusted God with his future.

Setting goals and living our dreams is not wrong, but missing life's moments while striving for achievement is never right. We don't know what tomorrow will bring, but trusting God today is the best preparation for trusting him tomorrow.

Are there any areas where you are procrastinating or not walking in obedience to the Lord because you are afraid of where he will take you? Prayerfully choose to embrace the moments today, trusting God for your tomorrow.

JEN BAKER

The risk of riches

You have indulged yourselves with every luxury and pleasure this world offers, but you're only stuffing your heart full for a day of slaughter. (v. 5, TPT)

People have debated for centuries whether money is good or evil, necessary or a vice. In a world obsessed with pleasure it's perhaps challenging to remember that God is ambivalent about money, but he cares deeply about the heart.

There are some who have taken to a simple life in the mountains to avoid any obsession with possessions. Others declare luxurious living is a gift given by God to be enjoyed in this lifetime, not only as an inheritance in the next.

Personally, I don't believe God is remotely concerned with our bank balance, but he is greatly concerned when that balance affects our heart. When pleasure and self-gratification become our goals, we have misplaced his gift (see James 1:17) and what is meant to empower others starts implicating us.

In these verses James focuses on workers left unfairly cheated and people being badly treated, but these words are not limited to leaders who manage staff or run a business. All of us have opportunities to treat shop assistants, baristas or any other worker with dignity and generosity. What about offering a financial gift to someone who gives you free teaching through podcasts or social media? Maybe there is a young person who could use some extra help financially while they are studying at university? You could send your pastors a gift voucher to a nice restaurant in town or offer childcare to a young couple struggling with sleep deprivation.

Today, choose generosity, because there is a day coming when all that we have accumulated will remain as we relocate to a city already possessing all we need and more.

Lord, I want to be an outrageous giver for your kingdom. Please show me how I can be a conduit of your blessing in a world often fuelled by selfishness. Amen.

JEN BAKER

Watching our words

Above all, my brothers and sisters, do not swear – not by heaven or by earth or by anything else. All you need to say is a simple 'Yes' or 'No'. Otherwise you will be condemned. (v. 12, NIV)

In today's reading, James talks about patience, perseverance, not complaining and not judging – all of which are important topics. So, it may be surprising that he begins verse 12 by saying 'Above all'. In other words, what we are about to read trumps patience, perseverance, complaining and carrying a heart of judgement!

Surely he must be talking about the importance of doing everything in love or walking in integrity? Maybe he will spotlight the importance of obedience in a disobedient world? Nope. James foregoes all these to highlight the danger of embellishing our words!

In the eyes of heaven, not speaking oaths in times of delay is more important than not giving up in times of trouble. When we attempt to move the hand of heaven (or our spouse) by attaching 'God' to our words, we have stepped dangerously close to manipulation and control. People should know that we mean what we say without needing to super-spiritualise our words, and God will know that we trust him without needing us to say so; remember, he knows our heart better than us (Jeremiah 17:9).

As we near the end of our journey with James, we find him once again speaking about words and works. Are we striving to gain approval from heaven through the words that we speak? Could we be manipulating a conversation by adding spiritual language to strengthen our personal argument?

Years ago, a handshake was all it took to seal a contract. Wouldn't it be wonderful if our reputation for integrity was so strong that we never felt the need to justify or embellish our point of view? In a world increasingly motivated by self-interest, I want to be known as a woman who speaks truth regardless of personal gain. Will you join me?

Lord, it can be challenging not to manipulate and fight for my way in a world thriving on selfishness and control. Help me to stay true to you and only say what you want me to say, trusting you for the outcome. Amen.

JEN BAKER

Pray for one another!

Therefore confess your sins to each other and pray for each other so that you may be healed. The prayer of a righteous person is powerful and effective. (v. 16, NIV)

The depth of truth within these verses extends well beyond the space of this devotional. For centuries books have been written and theologians have debated the 'prayer of faith' and its link to confession, sickness and healing. Regardless of what you believe about praying for healing, notice how verse 16 begins with the word 'therefore'. In other words, what has been written prior to this is integral to what James is saying about confessing our sins and praying for one another. (You might want to go back and read those verses again.)

If we are one body in Christ (1 Corinthians 12:27), then we are intricately linked in the plans and purposes of heaven. Therefore, it makes sense to say that supporting and championing one part of the body can only be healthy for all the other parts. James is saying that confessing our sins to one another in humility allows our humanity to move out of the way, opening the floodgates for a prayer life that is powerful and effective.

When was the last time you confessed your sin to another person? In a world that thrives on filters and survives through power, we are hard-pressed to see heart-felt confession happening on a regular basis. I am not advocating a binging of our brokenness or becoming transparent to every person at church, but according to James the more deeply we share with one another the more effective our prayer life will be. Personally, I wish this wasn't the case(!) but the Lord is showing us this type of relationship brings a freedom that hiding will never achieve.

In summary, our prayer lives are not empowered by biblical knowledge and flowery words but through an open heart which believes sin can still be forgiven and miracles can still be experienced.

Lord, thank you for this journey through James and all I have learned. Help me to put down my defences and strengthen my trust so I can be a godly woman who uses her words and works to display heaven's wisdom. Amen.

JEN BAKER

Making the familiar unfamiliar

Hannah Fytche writes:

Whether you've heard it many times or it's new to you, the story Jesus told of the prodigal son is one to which we can repeatedly return and find something nourishing for our faith. Through parables Jesus invites us to think about who God is, who we are and what God's kingdom is like. Parables don't offer answers, but they do offer stories which provoke curiosity and lead us to new insights.

When it comes to familiar parables, it might take a little more work to think our way into new questions. If you're familiar with the parable of the prodigal son, you might be lulled into thinking you know the insights already – you've heard it many times, and you've explored it as much as possible.

The youngest son asks for his inheritance, squanders it and so returns home. He represents repentant sinners, those who disobey and return to God. The father, representing God, runs to welcome his wayward son, and shows a love which is so surprisingly forgiving that a feast is thrown for the sinful son. The eldest son is trickier to interpret but surely his anger is misplaced – he should be celebrating his brother's return. As for other members of the family's household, such as servants and women, they are simply not present.

This week we will question familiar interpretations of this parable, allowing our certainties about it to be unsettled as we ask whether the youngest son is *really* a sinner and whether the father's love is *really* so surprising. I have been helped in my understanding of this parable by Amy-Jill Levine's *Short Stories by Jesus* (Harper Collins, 2014), which is well worth a read if you want to take your questioning beyond this week.

Take this as an invitation to explore this parable afresh. You don't have to agree with everything I write. That's the gift of parables – through offering us stories rather than answers they take us on a wondering journey closer to who God is and who we are with God. As we explore, let's pray: *Jesus, with gratefulness we approach this parable. We bring all our questions and curiosity, trusting you to show us the way. Draw us into the wonder of who you are, what your kingdom is like and who we are with you. May this nourish our faith. Amen.*

Parables don't have titles

Jesus continued: 'There was a man who had two sons.' (v. 11, NIV)

Read through the parable. What captures your attention? What surprises you? What do you like? What questions do you have?

Look at what the parable is called. In most Bibles, it's titled 'The parable of the prodigal son' or 'The parable of the lost son'. These titles were added by the editors of our English translations. Jesus didn't announce a title when he told this story (he just 'continued' to speak), and the ancient manuscripts of the New Testament also don't include titles. Titles were added later to help us find our way through the text. Yet as well as helping us find parts of the Bible, titles can shape *how* we read the Bible.

When we read 'The parable of the *lost* son', we notice how the son is lost – the ways that he's strayed from home. We might compare him to the coin and the sheep in the other so-called 'lost' parables in Luke 15 (and that might mistakenly lead us to think that the son is 'found' in a similar way to the coin or sheep). When we read 'The parable of the *prodigal* son' we might focus especially on how the son is wasteful, risky, reckless.

What might happen if we called it 'The parable of the *found* son', 'The parable of the heartbroken father' or 'The parable of the elder brother'? It might change what we notice as we read the story. New things might be highlighted. Our familiar interpretations might shift and change.

If *you* had to give this parable a title, what would you call it? Thinking about what strikes you as the main theme recognises that new meaning can come to light. Through your response to the Bible, Jesus continues to speak.

Dear Jesus, as we bring our own perspectives to your story, show us themes that we might not have spotted before. Draw near to us in our curiosity, revealing afresh who you are and who we are with you. Amen.

HANNAH FYTCHE

The younger son did not sin

'Not long after that, the younger son got together all he had, set off for a distant country, and there squandered his wealth in wild living.'
(v. 13, NIV)

The youngest son asks for his inheritance early. Having received it from his father, he spends it all. Soon he's so lacking in funds that he dreams of eating pigs' food.

I've often heard the actions of the youngest son interpreted as sinful. This is partly due to the son describing himself as a 'sinner' later in the parable (we'll return to that tomorrow!) – but the case for the son's sin is also made on the basis of assumptions about the cultural context of Jesus and his listeners.

Have you heard it said that the youngest son's request for an early inheritance is an insult to his father, perhaps even *sinful* due to the dishonour it implies? Well – it might not actually be that shocking. While the youngest son's request might be unwise, Jesus' first listeners may not have seen the youngest son's behaviour as sinful or even as that unusual.

Have you also heard it said that the youngest son was sinful because he ended up among pigs, animals considered 'unclean'? Jewish New Testament scholar Amy-Jill Levine pushes against this: the son didn't eat or kill pigs; he fed them. The son did not necessarily become unclean by the standards of Jewish law – rather, his problem was hunger.

When we reimagine the parable along these lines, the youngest son is no longer a 'sinner' needing forgiveness. His poor judgement and misuse of what he's been given has led him to hunger. There is certainly something to be said about what he invests in and why, but his need now is food: in this moment the good news he's seeking is food rather than forgiveness.

How might this unsettle familiar interpretations of this parable? I wonder how your imagination of the youngest son is changing – or staying the same.

Jesus, I'm humbled by how many layers there are to reading the Bible. Please keep showing me who you are and who I am with you through how I'm imagining and reimagining the characters of this parable. Amen.

HANNAH FYTCHE

The younger son did not repent

'When he came to his senses, he said, "How many of my father's hired servants have food to spare, and here I am starving to death!"' (v. 17, NIV)

At the point of starvation, an idea occurs to the youngest son. Where might he find food? Back at his father's, of course! There everyone has enough, from hired servants to sons. He imagines he's lost his father's favour, so he concocts a plan. He'll declare his sinful unworthiness and ask for a job.

Yesterday we considered an alternative interpretation of the son – not as sinful, according to Jesus' listeners' understanding of sin, but as so unwise that he's in desperate circumstances. (This is not to say that all desperate circumstances we might find ourselves in are caused by a lack of wisdom – far from it. Just that for the youngest son this could be the case.)

Yet if the son is not sinful, why might he plan to declare that he has sinned 'against heaven and against [his father]' when he returns? One answer might reveal itself if we hear the son's words in a scheming rather than a repentant tone. Might the son be returning not because he's seen the error of his ways, but because he sees an opportunity for an easy meal back home?

Amy-Jill Levine suggests that Jesus' listeners might have heard the son's words as deceptive rather than repentant because of their resonance with Pharaoh's words in Exodus 10:16, which Jesus' listeners were likely familiar with: 'I have sinned against the Lord your God and against you.' Pharaoh's words are empty, and so may be the son's.

Imagining the youngest son in this unfamiliar light is a challenge. It contradicts the ways I've heard this parable in church, pushing me to be open to other possibilities and to dig deep into the Bible's context. I don't know what to make of the youngest son anymore: is he a character I can relate to, or find an example in? What is he really like? It's good to ask these questions, letting new knowledge unsettle previous assumptions. Take a moment to recognise the questions that you have about this parable.

Jesus, open our eyes to different possibilities in this parable. Show us how contrasting interpretations can help us to learn more. Keep telling us the story of you, provoking our curiosity and leading us closer to you. Amen.

HANNAH FYTCHE

The father's love is not surprising

'But while he was still a long way off, his father saw him and was filled with compassion for him; he ran to his son, threw his arms round him and kissed him.' (v. 20, NIV)

I love this bit: the father runs to his son. We often reflect this back to what we know of God: as the father is compassionate towards his son, so God is compassionate towards us. His outstretched arms embrace us.

Continuing to make the familiar unfamiliar, let's ask how our understanding of the father's actions changes if we see the youngest son as *deceptive* rather than repentant.

As I've considered this, what has struck me is how much *more* this shows the father's care. His actions are not dependent on the son's repentance: he runs before he's heard a word. He throws his arms around his child without knowing *why* he's returned. The possibility that the son hasn't come back with good intentions might be on his mind; he embraces him anyway.

I've also realised how much my understanding of the father's compassion has relied on portrayals of his actions as surprising. While the father's actions, as patriarch of the household, might have been undignified or dishonourable, they need not be seen as surprising. This is the father of a son whose life has fallen apart. Why wouldn't he embrace him? The father's love is not surprising.

Here we might want to relate to the youngest son, even though we've complicated his character by seeing him as unwise and potentially deceptive. I wonder if this gives us permission to recognise our own mixed emotions and motives as we turn towards God. Maybe we can recognise that there is more to God's unsurprising love than we expect: if the son's motives are mixed and his father still embraces him, perhaps we can bring *our* whole selves to God, and not just the parts that we think could persuade God to love us. All we need do is turn and see God there, arms already outstretched.

Jesus, in this parable we meet a father figure who loves his son without condition or question. May I turn towards you with my mixed emotions and motives, knowing that before I say a word you already love. Amen.

HANNAH FYTCHE

There were not only men in this story

'"Your brother has come," he replied, "and your father has killed the fattened calf because he has him back safe and sound."' (v. 27, NIV)

A feast for the returned son, with the finest food and a celebration of a family reunited! A joy. Yet – I've realised that when I've imagined this scene, I've only ever imagined men at the party. I've pictured the youngest son filling up on his first meal at home, his father standing nearby and his brother at a distance angrily holding a cup of wine. Other characters fade into the background, but they're a male crowd – the youngest son's friends, perhaps.

Where are the women? It's not that there wouldn't have been women. The sons would have had a mother or a stepmother. Women would have managed the household, hosted events and prepared the food. While no women are mentioned in the parable, the setting of a household evokes the presence of women. Why have I found myself only imagining men into the story?

I've asked this question of many Bible stories. Our imagination has been moulded too often around only male characters, partly due to the way that the patriarchal culture within which Bible texts were written has silenced women's voices, and partly due to the ways that our own cultures have embedded patriarchal perspectives in how we read the Bible. I'm on a personal mission to reimagine Bible stories with women present: was there a mother watching her boys at the party, surrounded by her friends? Were there sisters as well as brothers? What part did women play in throwing the feast?

Let this question unsettle how you imagine this parable. It's not a parable only of a prodigal son, a heartbroken father and an elder brother. It's the parable of a household, in which women would've contributed to the story's events. Let this reimagination affect not only this story, but also other Bible stories. What voices have been silenced, and how can we hear them anew?

Jesus, as I read your stories, help me to listen for the voices of those who have been silenced – women, servants or slaves. Rewire my imagination to amplify the stories of those who have been forgotten. Amen.

HANNAH FYTCHE

The elder brother's anger isn't misplaced

'Look, these many years I have served you, and I never disobeyed your command, yet you never gave me a young goat, that I might celebrate with my friends.' (v. 29, ESV)

The eldest son stands outside the party. His grip on his glass is tightening, white knuckles betray anger boiling up inside. How come his younger brother is celebrated after spending so much of their father's inheritance?

He sees his father approaching and every muscle in his body tenses. The last thing he needs is confrontation. As his father pleads, he feels the hot words spew out of his mouth: 'I have been faithful to you! And you have given me nothing.'

The elder brother is a really tricky character to interpret. I've often heard his jealousy of the younger brother as something to be condemned: he shouldn't be this angry over the celebrated return of his family member; he should learn to forgive as his father does. He rails against his brother, extending the description of his recklessness to include paying for prostitutes, not just the ambiguous 'reckless living' that the narrator of the parable uses to describe the youngest son's behaviour in verse 13. Was the eldest son embellishing the story to justify his jealousy? Perhaps.

Or perhaps not, and the youngest son's 'reckless living' did include what the eldest son describes. I wonder if the eldest son's anger is justified. I wonder if it's okay for him to feel deeply angry. I think there's value in allowing him to feel his anger honestly and to its end, later working out how to respond and whether to live alongside his brother and father.

You can see the possibilities for reading this part of the parable. It's complicated, open-ended. It's not always entirely satisfying. It raises questions about the father's character (how does the father represent God here, or not?) That's okay: remember parables don't offer answers, they offer stories that provoke curiosity. What do you make of the elder brother?

Jesus, give me empathy to hear the elder brother's anger. May I recognise the value in honest emotions, and may I use my own emotional experiences to help me relate to the characters in the Bible. Amen.

HANNAH FYTCHE

Unanswered questions

'"My son," the father said, "you are always with me, and everything I have is yours. But…"' (vv. 31–32, NIV)

The parable concludes with the father reassuring his eldest son that he'll always share in his father's life – 'Everything I have is yours.' This is the father who ran to embrace his youngest son. After their heated confrontation, I would like to imagine him looking deep into his eldest son's eyes, hoping to communicate the same depth of love as he shared with his youngest son in that emotional hug. But I'm not sure: it still seems unsatisfying that the faithful elder brother gets a confrontation while the wayward youngest son is honoured with a party.

Sometimes the gospels include Jesus' explanation of his parables – for example, with 'The parable of the sower' (or perhaps 'of the seeds', if we want to play with titles again). We receive no explanation of the prodigal son parable from Jesus. By placing this parable with the previous two parables in Luke 15, Luke gives us clues about how to interpret it: it's about celebrating the finding of what has been lost, the return of repentant sinners.

Yet we've engaged with alternative interpretations this week – we've allowed our familiar associations to be challenged. You'll hopefully have more questions than answers at this point. I'm wondering what happens next. Does the youngest son find a better way to live alongside those who love him or does he leave home again? Does the eldest son continue to resent his father?

I hope that opening up these questions has led you to think anew about how you read parables and how freeing it can be to bring your own perspectives and honest, creative questions to the Bible. I hope that through your curiosity you've found new ways of imagining the brothers in our story, heard voices that might have been silenced and have experienced the wonderfully unsurprising love of God through the complexity of reading this story.

Jesus, you unsettle me as I spend time exploring your teaching. Help me to keep exploring the many layers of your word and how it connects to my life. May this lead to new ways of knowing you and of living in your love. Amen.

HANNAH FYTCHE

The rise and fall of Solomon

Anne Le Tissier writes:

What comes to mind when you think about Solomon? His mother Bathsheba's unfortunate story, perhaps. The influence of his father, David, good and bad. His gift of vast wisdom and wealth. His building of God's magnificent temple. His other lavish construction projects. His fleet of trade ships and accumulation of chariots and fine horses. Or perhaps, his many wives!

Of all these things, Solomon is possibly most famous for his God-given gift of wisdom. It is legendary. It spanned abilities in administrative, economic, social and military affairs as well as in learning and culture. It prepared him to build God's temple and enhanced his international reputation. He collected and composed thousands of proverbs, with two extensive collections credited to him in the book of Proverbs in scripture (Proverbs 10:1—22:16; 25:1—29:27), while being named as the chief contributor to the whole book (1:1).

Whether we think first of his wisdom or another outward attribute, we're reminded that God looks at the inward devotion of the heart (1 Samuel 16:7). Therein lies the key reason for the rise – and fall – of Solomon's kingdom. For Solomon didn't always 'practise what he preached' or 'walk the talk'. His wisdom didn't teach him godly devotion or self-control.

Scripture records how Solomon 'sought' (i.e. enquired of) the Lord at the outset of his reign, a phrase later used to measure the faith of Israel's kings. But as he grew older, he became increasingly careless in his devotion. Leaving God out of his work, wealth and pleasures, however, proved incredibly dissatisfying (as his writing conveys through the book Ecclesiastes). Moreover, it was devastating to the future of Israel. In 1 Kings 9:25 we read that Solomon fulfilled the obligatory three visits to the temple for major feasts, but we never again read of his pursuit of God's presence; a longing for God that David, despite his faults, maintained throughout his lifetime. Sadly, after many years, Solomon shipwrecked his God-given potential for himself, his son – and the nation.

We may enjoy and be inspired by 'rags to riches' stories, but we can also learn from the sadness of Solomon's 'riches to rags': his kingdom that rose to great heights, then fell. We can heed its warnings but also let it bolster our faith and rekindle our passion for God and his kingdom life today.

A vision to aspire to

Endow the king with your justice, O God, the royal son with your righteousness. (v. 1, NIV)

As we begin to reflect on Solomon's rise and fall as Israel's king, I invite you to join me in casting a wide-lens view over the life you still hope to live; even if you feel you have fewer years ahead of you than behind you. Look at the broad brushstrokes rather than the fine detail, at the characteristics and overarching principles you aspire to. For example, to nurture increasing knowledge of and devotion to God; to be a trustworthy friend; to be a helping hand to the needy. What might be your desires?

It's this broad vision of the nature of kingship that Solomon prays about in Psalm 72. Quite likely written for his coronation, or to celebrate anniversaries of his accession, the psalm asks God for an enduring reign (vv. 5, 15, 17), a practical impossibility for a mortal man, of course, but commonplace extravagant royal terminology (see Daniel 6:21, for example) and one that foreshadows the eternal reign of the Messiah. Our interest today, however, is in Solomon's request for God's help to be the kind of king he envisioned himself to be. Solomon's sensitive requests to be endowed with God's justice for the poor and needy and for God's righteousness and compassion are admirable (vv. 1–4, 12–14). Sadly, however, his life would prove how he spoke more wisely about the type of king he aspired to be than he was ever to live out in practice.

I'm convicted that I often set goals without identifying steps to keep me on the path to fulfil them. Join me in praying today for help from God to become the women he has still envisioned us to be.

Gracious Father, please envision my heart with how my life can grow to be more like Jesus and how I can live that out in practice. Amen.

ANNE LE TISSIER

God's name for you

She gave birth to a son, and they named him Solomon. The Lord loved him; and because the Lord loved him, he sent word through Nathan the prophet to name him Jedidiah. (vv. 24–25, NIV)

My parents chose my name, Anne, because they liked it, not because of its Hebrew meaning, 'grace' or 'gracious'. Names in Bible times, however, were often chosen to express a parent's desire for their child or a role God purposed for them. In fact, God would sometimes change someone's name in adulthood to reflect this; for example, Abraham and Peter (Genesis 17:1–5; John 1:42).

Solomon's parents came together through an adulterous relationship, enforced by David whose power would have dismissed any potential resistance from Bathsheba, who subsequently lost her first husband through David's murderous scheming, and then her child. I haven't space to unpack their story (see 2 Samuel 11), but the life or death of their second child must have worried them throughout her pregnancy. They named him Solomon, meaning 'peace', expressing their longing for him to know peace with God and peace in life. God graciously responded by giving the child another name: Jedidiah, meaning 'beloved of God' or 'God is a friend'. Although it wasn't used among people, it was sacred to God's loving purpose for him to live with the peace and prosperity his parents hoped for.

You may or may not like the name you were given. It may or may not hold significance for your life beyond it being a parental favourite or the name of a grandparent, for example. However, you may have adopted other names, wittingly or subconsciously, and today God reminds you of his names for you, the identity he's given you – the truth of who you are – in Jesus. If you've assumed the name 'rejected', receive God's name 'accepted'. If you've assumed the name 'unlovable', receive his name 'beloved'. What named truth from God's word might you need to adopt today?

Loving God, I receive and embrace your true names for me: forgiven, cared for, holy, blessed, chosen, victorious. Please bring to mind the name you wish to sow in my soul today. Amen.

ANNE LE TISSIER

God's promise will prevail

'My lord, you yourself swore to me your servant by the Lord your God: "Solomon your son shall become king after me, and he will sit on my throne." But now Adonijah has become king, and you, my lord the king, do not know about it.' (vv. 17–18, NIV)

While worshipping Jesus with Youth with a Mission in New Zealand, I was surprised to feel a tap on my shoulder. It was our tutor, sharing a prophetic word that God would anoint me with the anointing she had to teach his word. A few months later, I returned home to work, then to marriage and motherhood. It would be many years before God's promise was fulfilled.

We know little of Solomon's upbringing except that he was brought up in a complex, divided environment, with elder brothers vying for their father's throne. First, Absalom (see 2 Samuel 15:1—19:8), then Adonijah, but God had promised David that Solomon would succeed him. This wasn't merely Nathan and Bathsheba's wish (see 1 Chronicles 22:9), and God's promise prevailed despite his brothers' shenanigans, for as Solomon later wrote: 'Many are the plans in a person's heart, but it is the Lord's purpose that prevails' (Proverbs 19:21).

Solomon's rise to power was in God's hands, not the hands of his family or the nation's fickle commitment to one man then another. Nathan and Bathsheba were certainly instrumental in the unravelling of events, but ultimately they were protecting God's promise and therefore ensuring it would be fulfilled.

What has God promised you in his word or through prophecy? If circumstances have sown seeds of doubt over its fulfilment, be open to God about this. Sometimes we may be at fault for taking scripture out of context or for failing to test a message that was merely someone's kind hopes for us. But if you're assured this promise is a Spirit-breathed word into your life, be patient yet expectant for its fulfilment. Yield to how God is preparing you – in character or through developing skills and gifts, for example – but trust for its fulfilment in his perfect time.

What promise in God's word or spoken over you are you reminded of today? Have circumstances or the actions of others caused you to doubt its fulfilment? Pray about this with an open heart to receive God's encouragement.

ANNE LE TISSIER

Observe and prosper

When the time drew near for David to die, he gave a charge to Solomon his son… 'Observe what the Lord your God requires: walk in obedience to him, and keep his decrees and commands… Do this so that you may prosper in all you do and wherever you go.' (vv. 1, 3, NIV)

At primary school I gained 'stars' or 'house points' as a reward for work well done or for exceptionally kind behaviour. At home I was occasionally rewarded a little pocket money for completing extra chores. As adults we might hope for the reward of promotion for conscientious work that achieves set profits and targets. The reward of prosperity David offered Solomon is rather different.

For Solomon's throne to rise (i.e. to prosper), David charged him to 'observe' God's commands and 'walk' in his ways (v. 3). Unlike the second promise of verse 4, which was reserved for the royal dynasty, David's first instruction applied to all people, a promise simply reemphasising Mosaic law (for example, see Deuteronomy 29:9; 30:15–20). However, it was also David's instruction to ensure the rise of Solomon's kingdom. If Solomon were to step outside the boundaries of God's ways, he would be walking away from God's promised blessings.

We cannot earn God's favour and blessing; rather we're urged to align our lives to live within its parameters. Many people are gifted with wealth and affluence who've not received God's grace, so let's not confuse our understanding of prosperity with theirs. To prosper is literally to walk in step with God's ways that guide us in how to live the holy and fulfilled life he created for us, in harmony with his character and purposes. Such a life, in turn, grows his fruit and fulfils his purposes.

In our longing to nurture deeper relationship with God, to reflect Jesus more truly and to enjoy a greater experience of Christ's promised 'life to the full' (John 10:10), we too are charged to choose God's way of life, to live within the boundaries of his character and commands. How might you respond to that today?

Holy Father, please show me where I am stepping beyond the boundaries of your love, grace, mercy, humility, compassion and generosity, or any other way I am distancing myself from the blessed life you have for me. Amen.

ANNE LE TISSIER

33

Dealing with enemies

'You know in your heart all the wrong you did to my father David. Now the Lord will repay you for your wrongdoing'… and [Benaiah] went out and struck Shimei down and he died. The kingdom was now established in Solomon's hands. (vv. 44, 46, NIV)

Abraham Lincoln purportedly said, 'The best way to get rid of your enemies is to make them your friends.' If we offer and ask for forgiveness, speak well of those who've hurt us and seek to love them in action, friendship may be possible instead of animosity. Other times, however, attempts at reconciliation may be refused.

Solomon's succession wasn't entirely smooth, casting a shadow over its potential success. His elder brother Adonijah had recently failed to usurp David's throne, but appeared to submit to Solomon's authority (1 Kings 1:52–53). When, however, he subsequently asked for Abishag to be his wife, the woman who'd attended David in his old age (1 Kings 1:1–4), Solomon perceived the pretence as Adonijah's second attempt on his throne and eradicated his treachery (vv. 22–25). Abiathar's support of Adonijah was disciplined by removing him from the priesthood (1 Kings 1:7, 19; 2:26–27), while Joab's murderous behaviour was punished with immediate effect (vv. 5–6; 28–33). Shimei's curses were pardoned too, provided he remained in Jerusalem. When he broke his agreement, Solomon could no longer trust him, and he too was struck down (vv. 8–9; 36–46). It isn't easy reading, but the removal of opponents was customary for kings, and reprisals for rebellion a necessary punishment. For his throne to rise, Solomon had to deal with his enemies.

To continue growing into Christ's likeness and purpose, we're encouraged to make friends of our enemies (Matthew 5:43–48). If trust is broken, however, we may have to step away, forgiving but setting godly boundaries to protect our health and well-being from hostile behaviour. We keep the door of our lives open to love them, but without putting ourselves or others at risk.

Loving God, may I always convey the grace you've shown me to others. Where I need to humbly step back from evil, please guard my heart from being hardened through the power of your grace and love. Amen.

ANNE LE TISSIER

A stitch in time saves nine

Solomon showed his love for the Lord by walking according to the instructions given him by his father David, except that he offered sacrifices and burned incense on the high places. (v. 3, NIV)

An old saying teaches that 'a stitch in time saves nine'. In other words, it's best to solve a problem immediately to prevent it becoming a larger one; wise advice that Solomon could have benefited from.

Solomon was married to Naamah from Ammon and had a young son when he succeeded David's throne (compare 1 Kings 11:42 with 14:21). Early in his reign, however, he made an alliance with the king of Egypt by marrying his daughter (3:1). Arranged marriages to confirm international treaties were common in the Near East, but violated God's commands concerning foreign wives, whose worship of pagan gods might lure their husbands away from Yahweh (11:1–2). So, although Solomon's loyalty to many of God's commands 'showed his love for the Lord' (3:3), his inconsistent adherence to worshipping God at legitimate places was his major and persistent fault from the outset of his reign – early signs of his spiritual downfall which would undermine his dynasty.

'High places' were cultic sacred places, such as a flat hewn rock with an altar for sacrifice. Prior to the temple being built, some high places were used to worship Yahweh (e.g. Gibeon). Early on in Solomon's reign, however, he began to tolerate mixed worship, abandoning pure worship of the one true God.

At this stage, the problem didn't rob him of God's blessings on his rising kingdom, but it prompts us to ask God to search our own hearts and lives. What ungodly habits, character traits or use of time and resources are we tolerating? If we leave them unchecked, how might they lead us beyond the promised boundaries of God's blessing? Solomon's life that began so magnificently ended in misery. Let's take heed of the warning as we determine to realign our lives with God's character and will.

Forgive me, merciful Father, for when I appear to walk in your ways while my heart is set on pursuing other gods, such as my ego and reputation, materialistic security, or satisfaction of my fleshly cravings. Amen.

ANNE LE TISSIER

What would you ask for?

That night God appeared to Solomon and said to him, 'Ask for whatever you want me to give you'… 'Give me wisdom and knowledge, that I may lead this people, for who is able to govern this great people of yours?' (2 Chronicles 1:7, v. 10, NIV)

Imagine God inviting you to ask for whatever you wanted. How would you reply, and how might that have changed over the years? Being older than some of you, I'm aware how God has refined my requests as I've aged (though I admit there's still transforming work to be done), so I am struck that as a mere 20-something Solomon had sufficient self-awareness to make such a rich and mature request.

It was while Solomon was worshipping in Gibeon, where the tabernacle and altar were kept, that God invited Solomon's request, one which God was pleased to hear and respond to. After all, he could have asked for wealth, possessions, honour, the death of his enemies or for a lengthy life, things I might have asked for at his age. Instead, Solomon admitted his inadequate experience to govern God's people and build his temple in the way God wanted without his wisdom to show him how. In fact, it was the subsequent use of his gift that affirmed God's favour on him: Solomon ruled wisely over a dispute between two prostitutes and 'When all Israel heard the verdict the king had given, they held the king in awe, because they saw that he had wisdom from God to administer justice' (1 Kings 3:28).

No matter how we seek to serve God, we cannot rely on our own intellect, resources or abilities alone. Godly wisdom is paramount to knowing when, what and how we can pursue God's vision to the best of our potential. Is wisdom something we need to bring higher up the list of our prayer requests? Let's seek God's wisdom for our relationships, responsibilities and even for how to rest, an important necessity for a godly life.

God's wisdom is within us through his indwelling Spirit. When we ask for wisdom, we can believe for it, because as we still our thoughts to discern his response and walk in his ways, he reveals wisdom to us (James 1:5–7).

ANNE LE TISSIER

Solomon's splendour

Solomon son of David established himself firmly over his kingdom, for the Lord his God was with him and made him exceedingly great… King Solomon was greater in riches and wisdom than all the other kings of the earth. (1:1, 9:22, NIV)

'Everyone comes naked from their mother's womb, and as everyone comes, so they depart. They take nothing from their toil that they can carry in their hands' (Ecclesiastes 5:15). These wise words of Solomon berate my worry about future financial security, words that are especially poignant from a man of great wealth. Wealth, as we learn, is not so much for our ease and security, but is God's gracious provision for life, as well as to help us serve him in our different kingdom roles.

When Solomon recognised his need of God's help to fulfil his role in a way that would in turn bless God's people and help them to flourish, he asked God for wisdom. God responded by giving him not only the wisdom he asked for but also great wealth which made him 'exceedingly great' in the eyes of the world. The wealth he inherited from David, alongside God's wisdom and favour upon his administrative, economic, social and cultural affairs, blessed Israel with great prosperity and prestige among the nations. Trade, taxes and tributes poured inordinate wealth beyond that of any other king into Solomon's purse, during a period some now refer to as Israel's glorious 'golden age'. Like the Queen of Sheba, I feel overwhelmed just reading about it (9:3–4).

While Solomon walked in God's ways, his kingdom rose to giddying heights of splendour. Later, however, Solomon would realise that without God, material wealth was meaningless, another theme he reflects on in Ecclesiastes.

God knows what we need (Matthew 6:8; Hebrews 13:20–21). Whatever wealth of resources or talents, big or small, that he's blessed us with, their true value lies in God being with us as we use them wisely to love and serve him, and in turn bring blessing to others.

God my provider, forgive me when I've treated material things as an end in themselves rather than a source of your enabling to help me fulfil your vision for my life and a means to bless others. Amen.

ANNE LE TISSIER

Reaching out for help

'The temple I am going to build will be great, because our God is greater than all other gods. But who is able to build a temple for him… Who then am I to build a temple for him… Send me, therefore… Send me also…' (2 Chronicles 2:5–8, NIV)

It's not easy for some of us to ask for help if we're naturally inclined to self-sufficiency. We may think it's a sign of weakness, a showing that we're not as strong as the persona we like to reveal. We may even feel a little too proud to admit that we need help. Asking may therefore be an act of humility but it results in the blessings of teamwork, relationships and community service that give God the glory instead of diverting it on to an individual.

Solomon inherited a vast wealth of resources for building God's temple, from David's giving from both the nation's and his own personal wealth, and from the Israelites' liberal gifts (see 1 Chronicles 22:5; 29:1–9). However, Solomon humbly accepted his father's appraisal that he was 'too young and inexperienced' to build a magnificent temple for God's glory without the help of others, even though God had specifically called him to the role. Solomon therefore reached out to Hiram, king of Tyre, for supplies of Lebanon's esteemed cedar, pine and algum wood, as well as skilled metalworkers, engravers, woodcutters and embroiderers to work alongside his own craftsmen (2 Chronicles 2:7–9).

Whatever the nature of our God-given roles, responsibilities and projects, Solomon reminds us that to serve and honour God's glorious presence, we can ask him to equip us with all that we need for doing his will (Hebrews 13:20–21). Part of that comes from the enabling of his Spirit to impart us with gifts to fulfil our roles; but because the Holy Spirit equips us in different ways, our enabling will also come from working with others who have different gifts to our own, so that together we may glorify God and make him known through what we do (1 Corinthians 12:4–11).

Thank you, creator God, that I don't have to rely on my limited gifts and resources to fulfil your will. Thank you for those whom I can support and who support me as we together serve your kingdom purposes. Amen.

ANNE LE TISSIER

Living temples

Then Solomon began to build the temple of the Lord in Jerusalem on Mount Moriah, where the Lord had appeared to his father David. It was on the threshing-floor of Araunah the Jebusite, the place provided by David. (3:1, NIV)

Some years ago, I visited a number of temples in Hong Kong and India, whose ornate and fragrant ambience served to worship the gods whose images were carved on exterior walls. Temples were built in the ancient Near East too, as symbols to honour a national deity. For Israel, however, Solomon's temple was also to be a home for their living God to dwell among his people.

Today's reading paints an exquisite picture of the temple's grandeur – its pillared architecture, lavish gold panelling, intricately embroidered curtain, and ornate carvings and furnishings, everything constructed and crafted according to detailed plans that God gave to David (1 Chronicles 28:11–21). Seven years later, Solomon completed its construction in accordance with God's specifications (1 Kings 6:38). The magnificence and splendour honoured God but also sought to draw others to know and worship him – a temple for sacrifices for all nations and a house of prayer (2 Chronicles 7:12; Isaiah 56:7).

These details may seem irrelevant to our lives because Christ's sacrifice nullified the temple's purpose, but Paul reminds us: 'Your bodies are temples of the Holy Spirit, who is in you, whom you have received from God… Therefore honour God with your bodies' (1 Corinthians 6:19–20).

Just as the Israelites took great care to uphold the holy nature of God's presence in his temple, we can seek God's holy ways of caring for his dwelling place in our lives. His word teaches of temperance regarding our fleshly appetites and reverence for his presence in how we use and adorn our bodies. It also encourages us to yield to the nature of God's character and fulfil his good purposes so that all we do and say would honour and make him known.

Prayerfully read or sing the lyrics of the song, 'Take my life and let it be', by Frances Havergal (1836–79). How are you inspired to rededicate your life to God as his living temple?

ANNE LE TISSIER

Man of prayer

'Hear the cry and the prayer that your servant is praying in your presence. May your eyes be open towards this temple day and night, this place of which you said you would put your Name there. May you hear the prayer your servant prays towards this place.' (vv. 19–20, NIV)

Solomon's kingdom rose from incredible advantages, including inherited wealth, God-given wisdom, his people's loving loyalty and peace from war. Perhaps God's greatest gift, however, was the influence of a passionate praying father while Solomon was growing up. Just before he died, David urged Solomon to walk in God's ways and, at least during the earlier years of his reign, we see Solomon's prayerful, reverent awe.

Solomon first proved himself a man of prayer at the tabernacle in Gibeon (2 Chronicles 1:1–10), in a prayer that thanked God for his steadfast loving kindness, that expressed humility and asked for God's continuing favour. Almost a decade later, we again hear Solomon praying in awed response to the cloud of God's glorious presence taking up residence in the new temple (see 5:13–14). Solomon responds with prayers of praise and he testifies of God's faithfulness (vv. 1–11). He asks for ongoing favour (vv. 16–17), then prayerfully dedicates the temple by interceding for all who would pray in or towards the dwelling place for God's name, Israelite and foreigner alike. Seeking God's mercy and forgiveness for individuals and for times of national defeat, drought, famine, disaster, etc. (vv. 18–40), Solomon then asks for God's revelation of himself to continue in power (vv. 41–42). His lengthy prayers are prayed on his knees with hands spread wide before the altar of sacrifice, in a posture of reverence for God and dependence on him.

I had barely any instruction in prayer while I was growing up, aside from learning the Lord's Prayer by rote for school assembly. Whatever our experience in prayer, as God's living temples we can learn a lot from Solomon's piety, dependence, gratitude, praise and intercessions. How do they inspire you today?

'Teach us to pray', the disciples asked Jesus (Luke 11:1). We can ask him to teach us too as we adapt prayers from scripture or discern his leading, devoting ourselves to fulfilling our role as God's house of prayer.

ANNE LE TISSIER

Sowing and reaping

'As for you, if you walk before me faithfully with integrity of heart and uprightness… But if you or your descendants turn away from me and do not observe the commands and decrees I have given you and go off to serve other gods and worship them, then…' (vv. 4, 6–7, NIV)

Parsnip seed cannot harvest tomatoes – it's a natural order of reaping what we sow that reflects our spiritual reality (Galatians 6:7). Ungodly behaviour won't harvest God's promise of an abundant kingdom life.

God made promises to Solomon while he walked with integrity and observed his commands (vv. 4–5), but also warned him of consequences should he turn aside from his decrees and embrace other gods (vv. 6–9). Solomon's task was to protect and maintain the vast territory inherited from his father and to centralise government. While fortifying strategic border cities and developing trade ships were important, Solomon's lavish tastes meant it took almost twice as long to build his palace than it did the temple, and despite his father's adequate provision for the temple's construction, Solomon found himself in debt. In handing over 20 apparent 'good-for-nothing' Galilean towns in payment to Hiram of Tyre, he offended his old ally (vv. 11–13) and likely caused resentment in the towns' residents. In fact, his subjects, who'd been 'very happy' at the outset of his reign (4:20), became progressively disgruntled by the burden of taxes required to finance his projects and the enforced free labour he required of them. (Verse 22 speaks only of permanent slaves, but Solomon forced Israelites to temporary labour; see 5:13–14; 2 Chronicles 10:4). These actions sowed seeds that would eventually divide and undermine Solomon's kingdom.

God longs to be in reconciled relationships with everyone and cares deeply for the poor and oppressed. Solomon was in prime position to convey this but, over time, pride of wealth and power hardened his heart.

We won't lose our salvation for sowing ungodly habits or treating others badly, but neither can we expect to reap God's blessing from such a life.

Merciful Father, thank you for the fullness of Christ's life that I can experience as I walk in your ways. I confess my ungodly errors and habits. Please help me realign my softened heart to your loving, gracious ways. Amen.

ANNE LE TISSIER

The fatal flaw

Although he had forbidden Solomon to follow other gods, Solomon did not keep the Lord's command. (v. 10, NIV)

I first confessed Jesus as my Lord in my mid-teens and was baptised soon after. Peer-pressure, sensuality and worldly aspirations, however, sadly led me astray, and by my late teens, I no longer attended church while I chased life's many temptations and false promises. Even so, I never lost my faith and God never let me go. When his Spirit convicted me of my wayward rebellion, I discreetly visited another church and found myself weeping before the service ended. I still thank God for the dear woman who gently took me aside to hear my confession, reassure me of God's loving forgiveness and help me rededicate my life to him.

David sometimes failed to follow God's ways too, but his heart never turned away from God, and when convicted, he was quick to sincerely repent. It's this element of repentance that we fail to see in Solomon and which undermined God's covenant promise for his dynasty (v. 11).

We were introduced to his fatal flaw last week – his marriage to a foreigner that God had expressly forbid. But Solomon didn't marry just one foreign woman: 'He had seven hundred wives of royal birth and three hundred concubines' (v. 3). Solomon's wives may have enhanced his political powers and satisfied his sensual appetites, but they undermined his wholehearted devotion to God as they led him astray to worship their gods (v. 4). No one is perfect, but Solomon's persistent rebellion against God's law had caught up with him and his kingdom would be torn from his family (see also 9:6–9).

The tragedy reminds us that we remain personally responsible for how we respond to ungodly temptations and influences, those that we allow into our lives and those which intrude uninvited. What or who will we choose today?

There is always hope in God's mercy and love for a sincerely repentant heart. Come close to God again in confession. Determine to repent – to turn back to his ways – and God will come near to you (James 4:8).

ANNE LE TISSIER

Inspiration from tragedy

'See, I am going to tear the kingdom out of Solomon's hand and give you ten tribes. But for the sake of my servant David and the city of Jerusalem, which I have chosen out of all the tribes of Israel, he will have one tribe.' (vv. 31–32, NIV)

I like happy endings. However, the only happy ending guaranteed in this world is the beginning of life in heaven's perfection with God. I'm sorry, therefore, that our study doesn't end on a happy note; it isn't the upbeat way I'd have liked to have concluded Solomon's story.

God fulfilled his forewarned judgement on Solomon through one of his officials, Jeroboam, with the prophetic backing required of any claimant king. The symbolic action of tearing away (v. 30) foreshadowed the breakup of Solomon's kingdom into ten tribes ruled by Jeroboam, and, for the sake of God's promise to David (2 Samuel 7:16), one tribe – Judah – ruled by Rehoboam, Solomon's son.

God promised Jeroboam the covenant favour and enduring dynasty he'd promised David and Solomon (v. 38), but Jeroboam didn't walk in God's ways either. In fact, both he, Rehoboam and the majority of God's people abandoned their devotion to God; they worshipped idols, sacrificed to pagan gods and engaged in 'detestable practices' (12:26–33; 13:33–34; 14:22–24). Solomon's personal failure cost him his dynasty, but also detrimentally influenced the commitment of God's people – and in turn, God's subsequent favour on them too.

Solomon's downfall is tragic after such a promising start. We reflect on it, however, through the lens of Christ, who fulfilled God's promise to David of an everlasting kingdom. We are saved by God's grace when we place our faith in Jesus (Ephesians 2:8–9). We cannot earn or lose our salvation through perfect or imperfect lives, but we do experience increasing transformation into Christ's likeness, spiritual and inward blessing plus fruitful living, as we walk in step with him, yielding to how he wants to work in and through us. May Solomon's story inspire us to pursue this marvellous truth.

Gracious Father, I love you and thank you for my life in your kingdom and your life indwelling me. I commit myself today to drawing closer to you, walking in your ways and serving you in any way you choose. Amen.

ANNE LE TISSIER

What the Bible says about family

Christine Platt writes:

We have a complex, fascinating and sometimes controversial topic for the next two weeks: family. This word might happily induce warm fuzzies in you, and if so I rejoice with you for that. Alternatively, and sadly, this word might remind you of deep-seated wounds and revive painful memories of trauma and unfulfilled hopes and dreams. If that is the case, I weep with you for that but encourage all of us to explore God's viewpoint.

The word *family* comes from the Latin *familia*, which means household. This includes servants as well as the kin of the householder.

Another broader definition is a group of people united by their common convictions, for example of religion or philosophy. People talk about the nuclear family – parents and their offspring – and the extended family – three or more generations in addition to a nuclear family, including cousins, aunts, uncles, grandparents, etc.

The Bible gives us illustrations of several types of family structure. There are those related by blood, marriage or adoption, and sometimes they include servants. A probable example of this would be the Philippian jailor and his household (Acts 16:29–34).

Lydia's family in Acts 16:13–15 presents a different set up. She may have been single, and her household could have consisted of some relatives and servants. Alternatively, she may have been a widow and had her own children living with her as well as servants and people who worked in her business.

It is possible that Lazarus and his sisters Mary and Martha were unmarried and formed a household between them.

Our wonderful God has an all-encompassing view of family, as illustrated in Ephesians 2:19 (NLT): 'So now you Gentiles are no longer strangers and foreigners. You are citizens along with all of God's holy people. You are members of God's family.'

This includes all those who trust in Christ as their Saviour – male, female, rich, poor, all races and ethnic backgrounds – all are related to each other through our one glorious Father in heaven. No believer is excluded or of lesser importance than others. There is a place for everyone in God's family. No one who puts their faith in Christ will ever be disinherited.

The greatest family

So now you Gentiles are no longer strangers and foreigners. You are citizens along with all of God's holy people. You are members of God's family… And the cornerstone is Christ Jesus himself. (vv. 19–20, NLT)

God started the history of humanity with a family: Adam, Eve, Cain and Abel. We know that didn't go well, but God has not given up on his original blueprint of how humans can best flourish. He is committed to the concept of family.

I've had the privilege of observing positive and joyous family life, and I've looked on in envy and admiration. I've also been on the receiving end of fractured relationships and experienced some of the hurt and despair those can bring. Even if our earthly family is less than ideal, those who trust in Christ still belong to the best family in the whole world – God's!

Gentiles (non-Jewish people) were initially excluded from God's family as the first revelation of God was given to the Jews. The original intent was that they would be the means of revealing God to the rest of us. 'The Lord had said to Abram… "I will make you into a great nation… All the families on earth will be blessed through you"' (Genesis 12:1–3). For many centuries the blessing didn't get passed on. Gentiles remained strangers to God.

Enter Jesus! Jesus 'brought this Good News of peace to you Gentiles who were far away from him, and peace to the Jews who were near', with the result that we are now all members of God's family (v. 17). There are many situations where Jews and Gentiles relate peaceably together; however, any hostility between Jews and Gentiles still seen in our world today can be overcome. This scenario gives hope for the reconciliation of fractured relationships in other families.

Our own families may well disappoint us, but God is our Father, and he delights in having us in his family. We are cherished, accepted and valued.

Father God, thank you that you chose me to be in your family. I honour you for being such a loving, caring father to me and giving me Christian brothers and sisters to relate to. Amen.

CHRISTINE PLATT

Adoption and inheritance

You have not received a spirit that makes you fearful slaves. Instead, you received God's Spirit when he adopted you as his own children... And since we are his children, we are his heirs. In fact, together with Christ we are heirs of God's glory. (vv. 15, 17, NLT)

Adoption is 'the act or process of establishing a legal relationship between a child and a parent other than the child's biological parent, thereby entrusting the designated adult with responsibility for raising the child' (**dictionary.com**). The adopted child has the same rights, responsibilities and privileges as any biological children in that family.

As a child I used to fantasise about being adopted. Maybe I was really someone exotic, like an Arabian princess. Little did I realise that later I would discover that I really had been adopted into an amazingly marvellous and exotic family – God's family, with millions of fascinating siblings.

One of the first truths that was impressed on me when I asked Jesus into my heart was to trust in the assurance of my salvation. I needed to believe that I truly had been adopted by God when I gave my life to him. I wasn't a guest or a foster child; I was legally adopted.

I'm still learning what all this means. For the purposes of this devotional, one thing it means is that I'm an heiress. I've already received forgiveness and a restored relationship with God, but there is much, much more to inherit. There is a place in heaven for me, where there is joy, peace and love in abundance. I will enjoy a richer friendship with God, Jesus and the Holy Spirit, unmarred by any memory of sin or attacks of the enemy. I won't be relegated to the back row of heaven, for I will have the same rights of all God's children to approach him. Even now Hebrews 4:16 tells me that I can boldly come to the throne of our gracious God, where I will find mercy and grace to help me when I need it most.

How deeply have you embraced your position as an adopted child of the Most High? If you have doubts, you could memorise today's verses and ask the Holy Spirit to impress them more fully into your mind and heart.

CHRISTINE PLATT

Growing into the family likeness

God knew what he was doing from the very beginning. He decided from the outset to shape the lives of those who love him along the same lines as the life of his Son… We see the original and intended shape of our lives there in him. (v. 29, MSG)

Family resemblances are common, not only in appearance, hair and eye colour, but also in character traits, interests and talents. I have friends whose family culture puts hospitality high up the list of priorities, and they've naturally carried on in that delightful way of life.

Spiritually speaking God chose 'to shape the lives of those who love him along the same lines as the life of his Son'. How does that work? Most of us recognise there is a deep chasm between our daily lives and that of Jesus.

Growing into the family likeness is a lifelong journey. Paul gives us a helpful summary of what a Christlike life should be like:

> *[God] brings gifts into our lives, much the same way that fruit appears in an orchard – things like affection for others, exuberance about life, serenity. We develop a willingness to stick with things, a sense of compassion in the heart, and a conviction that a basic holiness permeates things and people. We find ourselves involved in loyal commitments, not needing to force our way in life, able to marshal and direct our energies wisely.*
> Galatians 5:22–23

Note that it is God who brings these gifts into our lives. We have to cooperate with his guiding hand, but we cannot produce these qualities by ourselves. The initiative of becoming part of God's family and growing into the family likeness all stems from God. He chose us and he transforms us. Our role is to surrender to his leading on our journey. Some of these qualities only grow to fruition through difficult times. How often have I bleated: 'Jesus, please give me patience now!' Only later have I realised that patience will only get developed in me as I encounter annoyances and problems.

Father God, please do your wonderful work in me that I might steadily grow and become more like Jesus. Help me to be alert as to how you are transforming me day by day. Amen.

CHRISTINE PLATT

The awesome gift of children

You made all the delicate, inner parts of my body and knit me together in my mother's womb. Thank you for making me so wonderfully complex! Your workmanship is marvellous – how well I know it. (vv. 13–14, NLT)

When I studied obstetrics, I was awed by the reality that one egg and one sperm got together and multiplied to produce a gorgeous baby with characteristics of both parents. All that has to take place in the womb for the little person to mature and be ready to face the outside world is truly mind-blowing. Each of us is wonderfully complex and marvellous.

At times, however, the pride and joy of a newborn loses its shine for the parents when they are bogged down with nappies, vomit and sleepless nights. It's a huge job and responsibility to care for even one child, let alone several.

'Children are a gift from the Lord; they are a reward from him' (Psalm 127:3). Even though the child is a special gift to her parents who shoulder the lion's share of the responsibility and have the most fun, she is also a gift to the wider family and community. Who knows what plans God has for that baby? She may become a person of influence for the whole nation. All of us, whether or not we've had our own children, can say that we have in some ways received the miraculous gift of children from God. Mother Teresa said: 'The child is the beauty of God present in the world, that greatest gift to a family.'

Looking at our world through the eyes of a child can help all of us to see more of the beauty of God around us. Watching a child's wholehearted delight in a dandelion, a kitten or a splodge of paint reawakens our own appreciation of simple pleasures. A child's smile can lift our spirits from the day's frustrations and help us to relearn that important skill – how to play.

Thank God for the precious gift of children in your life, whether your own or other people's. Look to see what you can learn about their creator from those children.

CHRISTINE PLATT

Honour your father and your mother

'Honour your father and mother. Then you will live a long, full life in the land the Lord your God is giving you.' (v. 12, NLT)

This is the fifth commandment God gave to the Israelites when he had rescued them from slavery in Egypt. The land he refers to is the promised land, Israel, to which he was leading them.

Honour has several meanings: to prize highly, to care for, to show respect for and to obey. Some Bible scholars have enlarged this commandment to include other authority figures: governments, employers, teachers and so on. This commandment is reinforced in the New Testament (Ephesians 6:1–3).

God gave the ten commandments to the Israelites as they were about to embark on a whole new life. They needed these rules to protect them and guide them in how to live. It's natural to chafe against authority as we grow up, but instructions are most often given for our welfare.

Our relationship with our parents changes as we grow up, so as we do so we need to adjust how to prize highly, care for, show respect for and obey. It's obviously unwise to remain in an abusive situation if we have the power to extricate ourselves. We also need not obey if asked to do anything immoral or illegal. It's important for us all to be alert and to notice and seek to rescue any children trapped in those harmful environments.

No parent is perfect except God. Our parents are those who gave us life and mostly they tried to do their best to nurture us. Parenting is a tough job. All parents need support to create a harmonious family life. The African proverb 'It takes a village to raise a child' illustrates the importance of a whole community interacting positively with children so that they grow up in a safe and healthy environment.

If your parents are alive, are there ways you could honour them? Do you need to offer forgiveness and thank them for the positive role they played in your life? If they have died, are there ways you could still honour their memory?

CHRISTINE PLATT

A family opens its arms

[Lydia] and her household were baptised, and she asked us to be her guests. 'If you agree that I am a true believer in the Lord,' she said, 'come and stay at my home.' And she urged us until we agreed.
(v. 15, NLT)

At this time, Paul and his team were itinerant missionaries to the Gentile world, going from place to place without any fixed abode. They were mostly dependent upon other people's generosity.

Lydia was an outstanding woman, especially noticeable in the male-dominated culture of the day. She ran a flourishing business selling high-end textiles. Although a Gentile, she had renounced pagan gods and worshipped the one true God. She joined in prayer with the few local Jewish worshippers. It appears there weren't sufficient Jews living in Philippi to warrant a synagogue as a meeting place.

When Paul and his team shared the gospel with the group, the Lord opened Lydia's heart to believe. Her influence spread to include all of her household, all of whom were baptised. Her first action as a new believer was to open her home to the travellers. She did not take 'No' for an answer. She persisted until they accepted. Later in the chapter, after Paul and Silas had been released from prison, they returned to Lydia's home and encouraged the believers. Maybe Lydia's home had become the local meeting place for the new church.

I've received kind and very welcome hospitality when travelling in Africa as well as elsewhere. It's so refreshing to be embraced in the warmth of family life in an unfamiliar culture.

Lydia is an example of using what she had to bless others. She set the tone for her household's warmth and acceptance of strangers. I have not been blessed with the gift of hospitality – I find entertaining somewhat stressful – but, when I have opened my home, it has usually been a precious experience. I don't need to offer a *cordon bleu* banquet; something very simple offered in love will suffice.

Lord Jesus, giver of all good things, thank you for my home. Please prompt me in how to use it to extend your kingdom. May all who enter my home be drawn to you. Will you open their hearts as you opened Lydia's heart? Amen.

CHRISTINE PLATT

When families are broken

'I don't have a husband,' the woman replied. Jesus said, 'You're right! You don't have a husband – for you have had five husbands, and you aren't even married to the man you're living with now'. (vv. 17–18, NLT)

In most wedding ceremonies the happy couple promise to love each other as long as they both shall live. It seems they both sincerely mean it on that day – only very shallow people would have in mind divorce as a future option on their wedding day. It's inspiring to see older couples who've been together for 50 years or more still faithfully doing life together, having created a secure home life for their children, and sometimes grandchildren. Their example of loving perseverance is to be highly commended.

Whereas most marriages start off with high hopes and thrilling expectations, they don't all have a joyous ending.

We don't know what sort of wedding ceremonies the woman Jesus encountered at the well went through, but no doubt she hoped that each husband was the one who would love, protect and care for her. Tragically she faced continual heartbreak (vv. 15–18). In the male-dominated culture of the day, this would have been no fault of her own, as she would have been powerless when rejected by this succession of men.

Jesus knew her history and had compassion on her. He had an in-depth chat with her, contrary to racial and religious customs of the day. We later learn that her testimony about Jesus brought revival to her village (vv. 39–42). Her story gives hope to those who've suffered the pain of a broken relationship. All is not lost. There is mercy and grace to help us when we need it most (Hebrews 4:16).

As the family is the fundamental foundation of human society instituted by God, we can be sure that the enemy of our souls will be doing his utmost to destroy it. Let's be on our guard.

Pray protectively for young couples as they seek to build a godly family together. Take every opportunity to be compassionate to those who have been bruised and scarred by relationship breakdown.

CHRISTINE PLATT

When children rebel

Children, do what your parents tell you. This delights the Master no end. Parents, don't come down too hard on your children or you'll crush their spirits. (vv. 20-21, MSG)

Wouldn't it be wonderful and make life more peaceful and harmonious for all of us if children always obeyed their parents? However, it seems that one of the first words toddlers learn is 'No'!

Bringing up children is a rewarding and challenging task, demanding oodles of patience, loving commitment and sacrifice. However, despite some parents' best efforts of modelling respectful relationships and instilling godly values in their children, in some cases these young people turn away and create havoc.

Bible characters were not immune from this distress and pain. David's son Absalom is a vivid illustration of this (2 Samuel 15—19:4). Absalom craved his father's power and prestige. He deliberately lied about his father's motives and 'stole the hearts of everyone in Israel' (2 Samuel 15:6). He then mounted an invasion force to evict his father from Jerusalem while planning to murder him. His actions were the antithesis of familial duty and love.

David was heartbroken. He wept as he fled the city, but still trusted that God would restore the kingdom to him. His grief didn't paralyse him. He mounted a counterattack to thwart his son's rebellion, though he still wanted to spare Absalom's life. Even though he would not let Absalom get away with this treacherous behaviour, it seems he forgave him and loved him still. He put in place the necessary discipline but there was still opportunity for Absalom to repent and be forgiven.

The opposite illustration is Jesus, who, at the age of twelve, 'lived obediently with' his parents (Luke 2:51). The testimony of his teenage years was: 'Jesus grew in wisdom and in stature and in favour with God and all the people' (Luke 2:52, NLT). This must be the heartfelt prayer of many a distraught mother and father.

Father, you are the perfect parent. Please give wisdom and patience to those who struggle with unruly offspring. Protect them from the enemy's attacks and give them hope for a brighter future. Amen.

CHRISTINE PLATT

Sibling rivalry

Isaac pleaded with the Lord on behalf of his wife, because she was unable to have children. The Lord answered Isaac's prayer, and Rebekah became pregnant with twins. But the two children struggled with each other in her womb. (vv. 21–22, NLT)

Even before their birth, Jacob and Esau fought each other. Their rivalry was not helped by each parent choosing a favourite child: Isaac loved Esau and Rebekah loved Jacob. We can be sure the twins were fully aware of this favouritism, which would have reinforced bitter hostility between them. Jacob eventually had to flee the family home for fear of being murdered by his twin, having tricked Esau out of their father's blessing. For many years they were estranged. During this period of being apart, they missed out on countless family experiences they could have enjoyed together.

The redeeming feature of this story is that when they finally met again as adult men they were reconciled. Before they met, Jacob feared his brother's anger, so he sent gifts as a peace offering (Genesis 32). Then, when they did meet, Jacob bowed down to the ground seven times. He was no longer the deceitful, cocky younger brother, but a man of humility, desirous of peace. Esau reciprocated; he 'ran to meet [Jacob] and embraced him' (33:4).

What can we learn from this? First, parents should not favour one child over another. Second, it takes careful thought and a humble attitude to restore relationships after a breakup. Third, everyone misses out when there is an estrangement – the parents, siblings, their children and all other family members. It's too high a price to pay.

Paul gives constructive advice: 'If it is possible, as far as it depends on you, live at peace with everyone. Do not take revenge' (Romans 12:18–19a, NIV). We can't change someone else's heart or mindset, but we can change our own. Amazingly, both Esau and Jacob came together in peace even after treating each other so badly. Reconciliation is possible.

Are you estranged from any family members or do you know people in that situation? As far as possible, aim to build a bridge and don't let it fester any longer.

CHRISTINE PLATT

Caring for the family

Tell these things to the people so that they will do the right thing in their extended family. Anyone who neglects to care for family members in need repudiates the faith. That's worse that refusing to believe in the first place. (vv. 7–8, MSG)

In the western world, where many people are having fewer children, there will inevitably be individuals who, through various reasons, are left with few or no relatives nearby. This isolates them, leaving them feeling disconnected as well as facing possible financial and other needs.

I've been around families where their homes and hearts seem to have elastic walls. They embrace outsiders with joy and ease. I've also seen situations where the opposite is true. In some households their home is their castle, and the drawbridge is firmly in place.

Although these verses relate to family connections, we could say that the extended family also includes friends and neighbours, especially those in God's family. I confess I was shocked when I reread today's verse: 'Anyone who neglects to care for family members in need repudiates the faith. That's worse than refusing to believe in the first place.' Strong convicting words indeed!

It's tempting to think that someone else should look after elderly Uncle Harry or wayward teenager Sophie, but, as members of the human family, all of us can play a part so that the whole load does not fall on a few willing souls. So often faced with overwhelming physical, emotional, mental and material needs, burnout is common among carers.

The parable of the good Samaritan (Luke 10:30–37) illustrates genuine care. He saw. He had compassion. He acted. These three components are vital. Sometimes we are so caught up in our own world that we don't even see. On other occasions, we feel sorry but don't do anything about it. At our best moments, we see, have compassion and act to contribute towards meeting the need.

Loving Lord Jesus, there are so many distressed people around me. It's easy to feel swamped. Please guide me to which needs you want me to respond to and grant me a heart of compassion. Amen.

CHRISTINE PLATT

Messed-up families

God said to Jacob, 'Get ready and move to Bethel… Build an altar there to the God who appeared to you when you fled from your brother, Esau.' So Jacob told everyone in his household, 'Get rid of all your pagan idols, purify yourselves'. (vv. 1–2, NLT)

If ever there was a messed-up family, it was Jacob's. Jacob fell passionately in love with Rachel, but his uncle Laban tricked him into marrying Rachel's older sister, Leah, first and then Rachel. Not a good start for marital harmony.

In the culture of the day, giving birth to sons was the pinnacle of success for women. Although Jacob didn't love Leah, she excelled and gave him six sons and one daughter. Both of Jacob's wives co-opted their maidservants to help. Each servant contributed two more sons and Rachel herself bore two sons. There was jealousy between the wives, and one can imagine tension, stress and fights in the household.

Despite all this chaos and unhappiness, God chose to give these boys the amazing privilege of becoming the founders of the Hebrew people – the twelve tribes of Israel.

One of the most famous sons, Joseph, endured horrendous treatment from both his brothers and an employer. He eventually became prime minister of Egypt and saved the Egyptian nation and his own people from starvation through his outstanding management skills.

Jacob had learned to trust God. He obeyed God's guidance to go to Bethel and led his family and household to repent and turn from foreign gods. God then reaffirmed the promise he'd made to Jacob's grandfather, Abraham, and his father, Isaac, that he would make him a great nation, that all nations would be blessed and his people would be given the land (Genesis 12:1–3). To crown the privileges poured out on Jacob's family, in Revelation 21:12 we read that in the new Jerusalem, when God establishes his kingdom on earth, the names of the twelve tribes will be written on the city gates.

Merciful God, thank you that you are not fazed by messed-up families. I present my family to you and pray for your blessing in each life and our lives together. Amen.

CHRISTINE PLATT

Persevere, persevere, persevere

But Ruth replied, 'Don't ask me to leave you and turn back. Wherever you go, I will go… Your people will be my people, and your God will be my God… May the Lord punish me severely if I allow anything but death to separate us!' (vv. 16–17, NLT).

Naomi had everything going for her. She had a husband and was privileged to bear him two sons. Both got married, so she had every expectation of a happy life surrounded by grandchildren. A perfect family set-up.

However, her husband died, followed by her two sons. A massive disappointment. She had lost her whole future and was probably destitute. Adding to the pain was that she was a foreigner and there was hostility between the people of Moab, where she lived, and those of Judah, her home country. She must have felt utterly lost and alone, and, like many of us, she blamed God for all her suffering. Deciding to return to the land of her birth, she urged her daughters-in-law to remain with their own people and hope for happier days ahead.

I love that this story is included in our Bible. It's so real. Naomi was broken and angry, and that can happen to any of us. Even when we make good plans, none of us can guarantee a positive future. What we see in this narrative is that God provided a helper along the way. Ruth was exemplary in her love and commitment to her embittered mother-in-law.

We will all face family crises where we may be tempted to give up on relationships. Ruth shows us a different way. Nothing was going to stop her from helping Naomi to achieve her goals. This story has an almost fairytale ending. The two women arrive safely in Bethlehem. Ruth finds work and is able to provide for their material needs. A godly husband appears, and Ruth has a son. Naomi has a grandson.

Whatever our family situation, God can enable us to flourish if we trust him.

If you are in a difficult family situation, ask God to send you helpers and be on the lookout for them. If not, pray for others who are struggling and for those seeking to help and support them. Amen.

CHRISTINE PLATT

When the worst happens

Wash yourselves and be clean! Get your sins out of my sight. Give up your evil ways. Learn to do good. Seek justice. Help the oppressed. Defend the cause of orphans. Fight for the rights of widows.
(vv. 16–17, NLT)

When thinking about all the benefits and joys of being in a family, becoming a widow or an orphan can be the worst-case scenario, especially in cultures where there is no state help for them. We can take widowhood here to also encompass any women left without assistance, especially single mothers, divorcees and trafficked victims.

God's message through Isaiah is blunt and forceful. God is fed up with pious religion and endless prayer meetings when innocent victims are suffering. This is echoed in the New Testament. 'Pure and genuine religion in the sight of God the Father means caring for orphans and widows in their distress and refusing to let the world corrupt you' (James 1:27).

I've heard several widows and divorcees tearfully bemoan the reality that friends no longer include them in social events since they were no longer part of a couple. It's considered an awkward social situation. How desperately sad and unkind. No wonder God gets angry.

The plight of orphans, especially in war-torn countries, tears at the heartstrings. We can feel helpless in the face of such trauma. Let's thank God for charities which make orphans their special focus. They need all the support we can give them. It is not solely financial support that is needed, but also inclusion by caring friends and families. Fostering, adoption and mentoring are all ways to provide what is lacking.

Making provision in your will is another way of ensuring ongoing care for the needy. We have Jesus' example of providing for his mother after his impending death. He entrusted Mary to his beloved disciple (generally understood to be John), knowing that she would need support, having lost her eldest son (John 19:26–27).

Think through how you can assist the more needy members of your family and the worldwide family. Caring for widows and orphans is a high priority for God. Is it also for you?

CHRISTINE PLATT

SATURDAY 19 OCTOBER   MATTHEW 13:53–58

Lost opportunities

They scoffed, 'He's just the carpenter's son, and we know Mary, his mother, and his brothers – James, Joseph, Simon, and Judas. All his sisters live right here among us. Where did he learn all these things?' And they were deeply offended and refused to believe in him. (vv. 55–57, NLT)

If anyone had a troubled family life, it was Jesus. His babyhood was marked by the rage of the insanely jealous King Herod, necessitating fleeing as a refugee to Egypt. His mother knew his true identity but, as far as we know, none of his siblings believed in him and were sometimes actively hostile (John 7:3–9). As the oldest sibling, he no doubt became an uncle. Several times in scripture we learn about his love and enjoyment of children. How amazing to have Jesus as your uncle! However, his life didn't fit the norm. He never married nor had children of his own. He was also rejected by the people of his hometown of Nazareth.

Jesus' siblings were possibly embarrassed to have such an unorthodox and high-profile brother. It must have been painful for Jesus not to have the support of his nearest relatives and neighbours who had known him since boyhood. Even at the cross, it appears that none of his siblings supported their mother as she watched her son being murdered.

But there is a happy ending! After his resurrection, Jesus made a special visit to his brother James (1 Corinthians 15:7). His brothers were present in the upper room when Jesus' followers met together. We can assume they all repented and believed.

Imagine how devastated they must have felt about the opportunities they had lost through unbelief. They were in such a privileged position living in daily contact with God incarnate: eating, sleeping, playing, learning with him as their big brother. The people of Nazareth also missed out: 'He did only a few miracles there because of their unbelief' (v. 58).

Some of us may live with regrets over relatives who have died, feeling that we could have valued them more highly or spent more time with them.

Father God, thank you for forgiving me over past errors. Please help me to cherish the time spent with family members and to make the most of any opportunity to learn from and serve them. Amen.

CHRISTINE PLATT

Joel: hope for troubled times

Amy Boucher Pye writes:

When I was asked to write on the book of Joel, I agreed readily. I did so remembering my experience of writing a fortnight of notes on the book of Hosea – how God's mercy and grace felt all the sweeter for having worked through some tough and heart-wrenching passages. Then, when I came to read, ponder and write on Joel, I began to wonder why I'd been so eager! Thankfully I also felt the same joy of witnessing God's justice and mercy in this prophecy, of his promises of dwelling in and with us, of finding hope in troubled times. I hope you too will be encouraged and built up through immersing yourself in this book. We won't leave any bits out, even the challenging ones.

Unlike many of the other Old Testament prophecies, we don't know the exact time when Joel gave his words to God's people, although because he mentions many other prophets, he may have written it after them. Nor does he address a particular way that the people were sinning against the Lord; instead, his non-specific words of conviction and mercy could be applied more generally to God's people as they sought to honour and serve him. We don't know much about Joel himself either – all his book says is that he's the son of Pethuel (Joel 1:1) – but his name means 'Yahweh is God', and his message affirms that truth.

During the next seven days, we move from a 'day of the Lord' of reckoning in the past, as revealed through the swarms of locusts, to a future 'day of the Lord' when his armies will contend with those who fail to honour him. Yet although the Lord demands justice, he also bestows grace and love on those who return to him, rending their hearts and not their garments (2:13). Not only will he not withhold his presence from those who have a tender and contrite heart, but he'll fill them with his Spirit, so that his people will see visions and dream dreams of God's coming kingdom.

I hope you're excited to delve into all that God has for us through the book of Joel. Know that whatever you're going through, God won't leave you. He dwells with and within you.

Cause for destruction

What the locust swarm has left the great locusts have eaten; what the great locusts have left the young locusts have eaten; what the young locusts have left other locusts have eaten. (v. 4, NIV)

In recent years, we've witnessed natural and human-made disasters that have radically altered communities, whether through earthquakes, tsunamis or invading armies. For the people affected who survived the chaos but lost homes, livelihoods and loved ones, life will never be the same. Joel's prophecy from centuries ago reveals the effect of a similar life-changing disaster to God's people: the insect raiders who devastated this agricultural community. A swarm of locusts followed by young locusts – which need to eat shortly after birth – followed by yet more ravenous locusts leaving destruction in their wake.

After Joel names the losses to vines, fig-trees, pomegranates, dates and apples, he calls the people to lament: 'Mourn like a virgin in sackcloth grieving for the betrothed of her youth' (v. 8). They should despair, wail and grieve (v. 11). In doing so Joel gives them permission to cry out to the Lord with all their pain and questions. They need not hold anything back from their God.

When disaster befalls us, we often approach God with the question, 'Why?' That is, why did God allow this atrocity to befall us? Was he behind it? We won't fully be able to find answers to questions like this this side of heaven; we simply don't know. But as we will see in this short Old Testament book, although horrible things happen even to God's people, he remains close to them. He will restore them with plenty of food (Joel 2:26); he will repay them for the years the locusts ate away (2:25); and he will even put his Spirit in his people, dwelling within them (2:28).

We too can lament; we too can trust in our unfailing God.

All-powerful God, I don't understand why so many horrific things happen. I cry out to you for help, for hope, for strength. I know you'll never leave me. Amen.

AMY BOUCHER PYE

Summoning the ministers

To you, Lord, I call, for fire has devoured the pastures in the wilderness and flames have burned up all the trees of the field. (v. 19, NIV)

Those who lead God's people play a key role in passing along his messages – not only the words of hope and salvation, but also the more challenging ones that call people to repentance and atonement. However, when ministers become wrapped up in the cultivation of their own images or platforms, they may find it difficult to hear and share God's convicting words.

Through Joel, the Lord acknowledges the important role those who lead God's people have; they are the ones he empowers to call the masses to humble themselves before God, to mourn and to fast. Notice the active language that Joel employs: 'put on sackcloth'; 'come'; 'declare'; 'summon'; 'cry out' (vv. 13–14). He is speaking directly to the priests so that they will in turn urge the people into action.

If you are a church minister or in a leadership role in your church, how do you respond to this pressing invitation? Perhaps you could take some time to think and pray through how your ministry has been shaped over the years. Maybe you're due for a retreat or a sabbatical, as the pressures and disappointments of leading have eroded your energy stores or your confidence in God. If you are a church member, how could you pray for and encourage your minister(s)? A note, a gift, an offer of help – simple and practical things can bless our leaders in ways we perhaps wouldn't anticipate, especially when those gifts come without hidden agendas.

Whatever our role, we can all turn to the Lord, looking to him when the fire devours, the flames burn up the pastures and the trees of the field (v. 19). To him we cry out, sharing our sorrows and seeking his help.

God our leader, we turn to you in times of plenty and in times of need. Bolster the faith and beliefs of our ministers and leaders, that they would spur us on to follow you. Amen.

AMY BOUCHER PYE

A dreadful day

The Lord thunders at the head of his army; his forces are beyond number, and mighty is the army that obeys his command. The day of the Lord is great; it is dreadful. Who can endure it? (v. 11, NIV)

After Joel outlined the swarms of locusts, which indicated that the day of the Lord happened in the past, he now shares what will happen in the future: 'a day of darkness and gloom, a day of clouds and blackness' (v. 2). This time the invading army that devours and lays waste arrives at the Lord's hand, and the arrival of these troops is truly terrifying – they leap over mountains, charge like warriors, plunge through defences and climb into houses (vv. 5, 7–9). How do the people react? They cower, their faces turning pale in anguish (v. 6). Quite simply, it's dreadful.

We may not like this challenging passage, but we can't avoid it. We read that the Lord is grieved by the disobedience of his people and will send judgement on an earth-shaking scale. As we consider this passage, we can also look to the New Testament, such as Peter's letter: 'That day will bring about the destruction of the heavens by fire… But in keeping with his promise we are looking forward to a new heaven and a new earth, where righteousness dwells' (2 Peter 3:12–13). I wonder if in our embrace of everlasting life with God, we sometimes discount the impact of the judgement of the Lord.

I invite you to ponder and pray today about these mysteries, holding to God's good character as you think about the fallen world that we inhabit. Perhaps God might lead you to repent for not only your individual failings, but also for the sins of a nation or a people. As you press into the mysteries of a good God and a world that is not as he formed it, may your love for him be strengthened and renewed.

Loving and just God, I throw myself and my nation at your feet, humbling myself before you and asking for your mercy and love. May we secure your forgiveness and grace, and not what we deserve. Amen.

AMY BOUCHER PYE

A cleansed heart

Rend your heart and not your garments. Return to the Lord your God, for he is gracious and compassionate, slow to anger and abounding in love, and he relents from sending calamity. (v. 13, NIV)

After the doom we experienced yesterday, today's text feels like a fresh breeze on a sultry day. Our God may be just, but he's also a God of love and mercy, one who desires that his people return to him. He longs for true repentance, the kind that reverberates throughout our whole beings, not merely the lip service we may be tempted to pay. I've witnessed this kind of half-hearted apology from children – when they are sorry for being caught but not truly regretting their wrongdoing. Soberingly, I realise that I'm not immune to this behaviour either!

We can ask God to strike our hearts with sorrow for the ways we fail him, whether for our actions or our inaction. His Spirit will encourage us to leave behind the daily activities that preoccupy us, just as Joel called God's people to gather before the Lord, including the bridegroom and bride on their wedding day (v. 16). Taking time out, we can repent before God, truly humbling ourselves and seeking his forgiveness and favour. We can ask him to spare us, so that his name will be praised (v. 17).

If you have the time, why not ponder this text from scripture while engaging with it creatively? You might wish to draw a picture of your heart, asking God to show you if there is any wickedness within it from which you need to repent, depicting that in pictorial form. Then create a refreshed and cleansed heart, waiting for God to reveal his healing and his loving words and images that he has for you.

Know that God loves you and will give you a clean and pure heart with which to love him and others.

Loving and merciful God, thank you for showering me with your forgiveness. Spark in me the desire to purify myself before you, that I would have a clean heart. Amen.

AMY BOUCHER PYE

A God who restores

'I will repay you for the years the locusts have eaten – the great locust and the young locust, the other locusts and the locust swarm – my great army that I sent among you.' (v. 25, NIV)

God hears, and God relents. After the words of judgement that we found so difficult in previous days, this pivotal part of Joel's prophecy speaks of God extending his forgiveness and mercy to his repentant people. He's 'jealous for his land' and takes 'pity on his people' (v. 18). All of the action from here to the end of the book takes place in the future, as the Lord through Joel shares about a wonderful time to come.

The blessings will not only be for God's people, but also for the land and the animals within it (vv. 21–23). For an agricultural people without irrigation systems, the promise of rain – both in the autumn and the spring – would be life-enriching. In one of the most memorable passages from this prophecy, God promises restoration: 'I will repay you for the years the locusts have eaten…' (v. 25). The stripping of the fields and fruit will not be the barren inheritance of God's people. Instead, he will grace them with plenty of food as the 'fig-tree and the vine yield their riches' (v. 22).

Charles Spurgeon (1834–92) spoke of the mystery of God restoring the fruit of the harvest that the locusts ate. He noted that although we cannot have back the years themselves – 'You cannot have back your time' – yet 'there is a strange and wonderful way in which God can give back to you the wasted blessings, the unripened fruits of years over which you mourned.' What a hopeful observation when we look back with regret over the spoiled fruit we have experienced in various areas of life. God will restore and renew us.

God of grace and mercy, I give you my sadness over the losses of years gone by. Touch me with your transforming love and give me hope to trust in you. Amen.

AMY BOUCHER PYE

The gift of God's Spirit

'And afterwards, I will pour out my Spirit on all people. Your sons and daughters will prophesy, your old men will dream dreams, your young men will see visions. Even on my servants, both men and women, I will pour out my Spirit in those days.' (vv. 28–29, NIV)

Not only will God restore the land, but he'll also renew his people with the best gift ever – his indwelling Spirit. He promises through Joel to pour out his Spirit on all people, that they would prophecy and see visions (v. 28). With God's Spirit within, they will be empowered to bless others, to share God's freeing words, to speak life into those whom they meet.

We see this prophecy fulfilled on the day of Pentecost. After the Holy Spirit came and people started speaking in other languages, some observers criticised them, saying that they'd had too much wine to drink (Acts 2:13); but Peter refutes them. He quotes from this passage of Joel, explaining that what they are witnessing is the fulfilment of God's promises to pour out his Spirit on believers (Acts 2:16–21).

If we believe in God, then he's filled us with his Spirit – and this makes all the difference to how we live and move and have our being. Day by day we will bear the fruit of the Spirit – our lives will be marked with joy, peace, forbearance, kindness, goodness, faithfulness, gentleness and self-control (see Galatians 5:22–23). We too will have words of knowledge for other believers, offering them in love and grace. We will collaborate with God in our work, bringing forth truth and beauty.

I invite you to spend some time asking God to wake you up to his Spirit dwelling within, that today you may heed his nudges and prompts. At the end of the day, before you go to sleep, review the day with God and notice where this glorious partnership brought forth fruit. What a joy to be empowered by God's Spirit!

God whose Spirit lives within, bless others through me, whether through an act of service, a prayer of intercession or an encouraging word. I want to spread your love and your life this day. Amen.

AMY BOUCHER PYE

God with us

'Then you will know that I, the Lord your God, dwell in Zion, my holy hill. Jerusalem will be holy; never again will foreigners invade her. In that day the mountains will drip new wine, and the hills will flow with milk.' (vv. 17–18, NIV)

Old Testament prophecies, such as this one of Joel, often have a two-pronged fulfilment. For instance, God's promise here that he will 'restore the fortunes of Judah and Jerusalem' (v. 1) occurred when God's people returned from exile in Babylon. As we look ahead to more long-ranging realisation of God's promises, such as the coming of Jesus and our life in the kingdom of God, we shouldn't ignore these more immediate graces for God's people.

While God promises restoration and his presence, he also speaks to the justice he will wield against the nations who made his people suffer. The words can make us cower: 'I will swiftly and speedily return on your own heads what you have done' (v. 4). This statement reminds us that we serve a God of justice, one who will right the wrongs committed against those who follow him. He is a God of mercy who bears our sins and wrongdoing through the death of his Son Jesus, but in our eagerness to accept his gifts we sometimes may overlook the deep cost of that mercy.

Think back over this past week and all that you've encountered in the book of Joel. As you consider which parts spoke to you most deeply, ask God to help you take into next week and beyond any words of wisdom or promise that will empower you to trust and serve him better. You may also wish to read verses 17 through to 21 slowly and meditatively, asking God to drip the honey from them deep into your being.

Know that the final words of this book hold true for us today – God dwells with us. What a glorious promise, whatever trials we are experiencing.

Loving God, you promise never to leave me. Help me to hold on to your promises when I suffer and am afraid. I want to be made holy, and I want to be with you always. Amen.

AMY BOUCHER PYE

A psalm for every season

Tracy Williamson writes:

When I was asked about writing a 14-day series on the psalms, I felt both delighted and humbled in equal measure. Who was I to think I could adequately unlock the depths of these wonderful writings in just 14 short notes? Knowing I'd only be able to use a few of the 150 psalms, how could I even choose which to use?

I should have simply prayed, because if there is one thing that all the psalms emphasise, it's that we can pray to God about everything. He is always listening and longing for us to go deeper in our walk with him – to hear his voice, to trust in his forgiveness and to grow in our understanding and worship.

I believe God guided me as to which psalms to use and what to bring out from them, and I hope that during this coming fortnight you'll find yourself on a journey of discovery and joy.

I've been exploring the very griefs and longings of King David, the sons of Korah and others. They wrote about facing disillusionment, loss, fear, rejection and loneliness – huge issues that we all experience at some time or another. It's mind-blowing that I found so much that is relevant and vital for every one of us today. The joy they wrote about is not a sugary sentiment but comes through discovering that, however we feel and whatever is going on in our lives, we can rejoice in the God who loves us and is always there for us.

We all have our favourite psalms, and you may find some of those you love in the following pages. It's my prayer that even if I've used a psalm that you're very familiar with, you'll receive something life-giving as you reflect on it afresh. Some of the psalms I have chosen may be new to you or ones you rarely read, in which case I hope you will be inspired to read them more closely and to seek God's message for you.

Writing these studies has taken me on my own rollercoaster journey and shown me I have much more to discover in God and much yet to experience in my prayer life. That's a good realisation, because God has called us all on a journey to discover more of him that will lead us to eternity.

Be blessed as you read.

Hope in disillusionment

Surely in vain I have kept my heart pure and have washed my hands in innocence. All day long I have been afflicted… When I tried to understand all this, it troubled me deeply till I entered the sanctuary of God. (vv. 13–14, 16–17, NIV)

I had planned to start on a happy note but was drawn to Psalm 73 and its theme of disillusionment. Here, Asaph describes a spiritual disenchantment because of the prosperity of the wicked as opposed to the struggles of the righteous.

Disillusionment and loss of hope seem to be widespread and can be paralysing. They drain us of joy and purpose and feed us with bitterness. If left unchecked, disillusionment corrodes all our communications with others and even with God. The trouble is disillusionment can sneak up on us without us realising. A dear friend of mine was struggling with severe pain. Despite many people praying for her, she worsened, and I felt helpless. God seemed far away, and I felt a churning anger at him. How could a God of love allow his children to suffer so? Disillusion crept in.

Like Asaph, we must face our feelings honestly, and his psalm teaches us how to do that. He says, 'When I tried to understand all this, it troubled me deeply till I entered the sanctuary of God' (vv. 16–17).

What was that sanctuary? More than any physical location, the sanctuary represents our own hearts. Revelation about his own place in God's heart came to Asaph in the quiet place of prayer. 'Whom have I in heaven but you?' (v. 25) he cries, as God whispers heavenly insights that dissipate his despair and give him strength and hope for the future.

We all need to enter that sanctuary. When I told God about my anger, I sensed his comfort and everlasting love for my friend. He is not distant from our pain; Jesus carries it as he walks alongside us.

God says: 'My child, I know your confusion, but I am the living hope and I want you to renew your trust in me. I will never leave or forsake you. Open your heart to my whisper and receive my peace.'

TRACY WILLIAMSON

Whom shall I fear?

My heart says of you, 'Seek his face!' Your face, Lord, I will seek. Do not hide your face from me… you have been my helper. Do not reject me or forsake me, God my Saviour. Though my father and mother forsake me, the Lord will receive me. (vv. 8–10, NIV)

Are you a fearful person? I am, and when I feel afraid, I feel paralysed, unable to think clearly or retain my peace.

David is clearly realising his need to cling on to God in the face of challenging circumstances. Focusing on God's character is key in our battle against fear. David declares confidently: 'The Lord is my light' (v. 1). Dark thoughts may grip us, but God is light, and that light is his love. He is our refuge.

Life can be very scary as we become aware of the brokenness in society and the effects of our own wounds. We need that refuge just as David did. David appears to feel rejected by his parents, but again affirms the truth that will bring healing and peace: 'the Lord will receive me' (v. 10).

Our fears may seem mundane but they can nonetheless cripple us. I feared frying an egg for my mum once, as she'd been so critical of me as a child. Now she was ill and needed me, but I was sure I would mess it up. I prayed, 'Lord, get me out of this,' but he said: 'Do it with me. I will help you.' He was, in effect, telling me to 'seek his face' and encouraging me that I would see his goodness. The egg was perfect, and mum even thanked me – it was the first time she had ever done that! God's love and help are so real.

David says, 'Be strong and take heart and wait for the Lord' (v. 14). There are so many ways he wants to make us full of praise instead of fear. Choosing to be with him and listening to his voice are vital. I long to grow in that same heart-confidence as David and to experience God's goodness and love every day.

Lord, I draw close to hear your voice. Thank you for being my friend and releasing me to know the joy of praising you even when I am afraid. I trust in your love and care of me. Amen.

TRACY WILLIAMSON

Are you on pilgrimage?

Blessed are those whose strength is in you, whose hearts are set on pilgrimage. As they pass through the Valley of Baka, they make it a place of springs; the autumn rains also cover it with pools. They go from strength to strength, till each appears before God in Zion. (vv. 5–7, NIV)

This beautiful psalm speaks of longing for connection with God: 'How lovely is your dwelling-place' (v. 1). Do we realise that we are his dwelling-place? God has chosen to make his home in our hearts. He makes us lovely with the loveliness of Jesus. Understanding this is vital because it leads us into true intimacy with God.

Where do we feel most free? I share a home with my lovely friend, Marilyn, and feel relaxed there. God longs for us to feel even more at home with him. 'Blessed are those who dwell in your house; they are ever praising you' (v. 4). I realise that sometimes I praise out of duty, but the psalmist shows us that true praise will flow as we live close to the one who calls us beautiful.

I desire many things, but the psalmist says, 'Blessed are those whose strength is in you' (v. 5). Is God the one you cling to, or do you seek different experiences, even though you know their effect will only be fleeting?

We all have longings, but the psalmist correctly identifies his inner restlessness as something that only God can fulfil: 'My heart and my flesh cry out for the living God' (v. 2).

To me, a key word is 'pilgrimage', referring to us seeking to grow and move forward in our life journey. Even very hard times – 'Baka' (v. 6) – can be transformed from hopelessness to joy if we know that God is constantly working within us and wanting to reveal new depths of his love. After affirming that just one day close to God is better than a lifetime without him, the psalmist rejoices in who God is to him, his power and protection, the deep affirmation and provision he brings. Such revelation comes as we trust God and seek him above everything else.

Father, forgive me for seeking fulfilment from everything but you. I choose to live my life in pilgrimage, constantly discovering your amazing love and greatness. You alone are my strength, and I will rest in you. Amen.

TRACY WILLIAMSON

Growing in joy

The Lord is gracious and full of compassion, Slow to anger and abounding in lovingkindness. The Lord is good to all, and His tender mercies are over all His works [the entirety of things created]. All Your works shall give thanks to You *and* praise You, O Lord. (vv. 8–10, AMP)

This is a psalm of joy and teaches us how we might experience more joy in our lives. David begins: 'I will exalt You, my God, O King' (v. 1). He chooses to reflect on God and his greatness. Personally, I can all to easily get pulled down by negativity, but David says, 'On Your wonderful works, I will meditate' (v. 5). He is focusing upon God's awesome character and ways, asserting that he will bless God every day. Do we have similarly grateful hearts? I can often take God for granted, but when I respond in gratitude, worship naturally wells up.

Throughout the psalm, David celebrates God's love of helping us. Recently, I was travelling by train, which can be tricky because I can't see the screens or hear announcements. I was worried that things would go wrong, and they did – the train I boarded didn't stop at my station. Annoyed, I prayed. A lovely couple helped me to get the right train, then a friend was driving past the station as I arrived and offered me a lift home. I could easily have forgotten that God was behind it all, but as I considered how he had 'opened his hand to help me' thankfulness and joy filled me.

This psalm also speaks of the impact of communal worship. David tells us that when others extol God, his own heart is inspired. It's awesome to take part in the major Christian events and festivals, where our praises mingle with thousands of others, but worshipping with others in a small group can also lift our spirits. In a workshop I was leading, I encouraged everyone to write some sentences starting with the words: 'I love you Lord, because…' The variety of reasons people loved him was incredible and created a beautiful psalm empowering us to worship and love God in a deeper way.

'I will sing to the Lord all my life; I will sing praise to my God as long as I live. May my meditation be pleasing to him, as I rejoice in the Lord… Praise the Lord, my soul.' (Psalm 104:33–35, NIV)

TRACY WILLIAMSON

God hears your cry

They confronted me in the day of my disaster, but the Lord was my support. He brought me out into a spacious place; he rescued me because he delighted in me. (vv. 18–19, NIV)

When the worst happens, we can be overwhelmed by a cacophony of fear, anguish and turmoil. David describes it graphically: 'The cords of death entangled me; the torrents of destruction overwhelmed me' (v. 4). He was in danger, alone, battered by the fear of his enemies. No one was there to help him, but he cried out to God.

Like David, we can often feel distraught and alone when life gets tough. Who can we turn to? David says: 'In my distress I called to the Lord; I cried to my God for help' (v. 6). What really impacts me is David's awareness that God was there for him, that he truly could call upon him. David had already spent endless hours worshipping God and building up foundation stones of trust in his love. 'I love you, Lord, my strength' (v. 1), he cries. Now in turmoil, he is sure that God has heard him. 'From his temple he heard my voice; my cry came before him, into his ears' (v. 6).

When we are in crisis, we too can know God's presence with us. God hears us. He knows our heart's cry. He sent his son to die for us because we matter so much to him. Call out to him and he will part 'the heavens and come down' (v. 9). David says: 'He rescued me because he delighted in me' (v. 19). Please know today that God delights in you, too.

Before I became a Christian, I was suicidal. One night I wandered away from my college lodgings and waded into a lake. I wanted to die and despaired when I failed. A week later, a fellow student invited me into her room and told me that God loved me. He had heard my heart's cry and my life was turned around.

He hears your cry today.

Thank you, O my Father, that you bring me out into a spacious place and enable me to walk on the heights. You make me more than a conqueror. You keep my lamp burning and turn my darkness into light. Amen.

TRACY WILLIAMSON

Following holy nudges

Listen, daughter, and pay careful attention: Forget your people and your father's house. Let the king be enthralled by your beauty; honour him, for he is your lord. (vv. 10–11, NIV)

I love how the psalms speak on so many levels. This psalm is celebrating King Solomon's wedding, extolling his majesty and might, yet beyond that there is the prophetic message pointing to the coming of Jesus and his betrothal to us, his bride.

God speaks through the everyday events of life just as he speaks through his word, hymns or the beauty of creation. Jesus said: 'Whoever has ears, let them hear' (Matthew 11:15), referring to our need to listen with our hearts for God's secret messages. The psalmist begins: 'My heart is stirred by a noble theme' (v. 1). When we feel that stirring, like a holy nudge, it's a sign that God is revealing something deeper than what we outwardly see. Here, it's as if he is seeing beyond the immediate glory of the occasion into heavenly revelation. Have you experienced that? I remember walking my dog on a miserable winter's day. It was very gloomy but suddenly a ray of sunshine pierced through the clouds and transformed the muddy grass to gold. I was stunned as in the holy stillness Romans 8:19 unfolded in my mind: 'The creation waits in eager expectation for the children of God to be revealed.' I knew God was saying that just as the grass had been transformed, so we who feel ourselves to be as nothing will be transformed by his Son; and as we realise we are his beloved children, we will impact the very universe.

My friend Marilyn was released into ministry as God highlighted the verses: 'Forget your people and your father's house. Let the king be enthralled by your beauty' (vv. 10–11). She'd feared her dad's disapproval but realised through these verses that she needed to honour God's call. She is still touching lives today with her music.

Thank you, Lord, for the many layered messages in your word. Thank you that you are enthralled by my beauty. Help me to live as your beloved, hearing your voice and seeing into heaven's realms. Amen.

TRACY WILLAMSON

Unashamed

Do not let me be put to shame, nor let my enemies triumph over me. No one who hopes in you will ever be put to shame… The Lord confides in those who fear him; he makes his covenant known to them. (vv. 2–3, 14, NIV)

Like all relationships, our relationship with God is multifaceted, but at its heart it rests on Jesus' forgiveness and love. As we stand on this truth, all his resources of power and love become ours. Psalm 25 reflects that journey. David starts with shame, something that ties so many of us in knots. 'Do not let me be put to shame' (v. 2), he begs. We feel shame when we become prey to the false judgement of others. Guilt says, 'You've done wrong.' Shame says, 'You are wrong.' I lived with shame because of childhood abuse. It controlled every part of my life. It seems David experienced shame through his parents' rejection (Psalm 27:10), and he is nervous that God will act similarly. But as he steps deeper into God's love, he is able to say: 'No one who hopes in you will ever be put to shame' (v. 3).

Are you walking that pathway of shame too? Let this psalm touch you. David asks God to guide him in his truth. Part of that truth is seeing who God really is. David discovers that 'all the ways of the Lord are loving and faithful' (v. 10). Speaking these truths out loud moves us from the fear of man to the reverent fear of God. This opens us to hearing God's counsel and experiencing his favour. David shares his beautiful revelation: 'The Lord confides in those who fear him; he makes his covenant known to them' (v. 14). His covenant – the fullness of his promises, the reality of his love, the freedom and joy he brings, his equipping us to do his works – is given to us.

You only confide in someone you trust like a close friend. God calls us such friends. Will we, like David, put our hope and trust in him?

A vision: I see you sitting with Jesus by a lake. He is joyfully pointing things out and delighting in your reactions. He is holding you close and treasuring all you say. A wonderful glimpse of how he cherishes your friendship.

TRACY WILLIAMSON

Created, known and loved

You formed my innermost being, shaping my delicate inside and my intricate outside, and wove them all together in my mother's womb. I thank you, God, for making me so mysteriously complex! Everything you do is marvellously breathtaking. It simply amazes me to think about it! How thoroughly you know me, Lord! (vv. 13–14, TPT)

Whenever I feel low, I turn to this psalm. It is a wonderful illustration of how God loves to give us deep revelation as we come into that secret place with him. David begins to perceive how vast and deep God's knowledge of him is – every thought, every action, every word all seen and known. That could be scary, but David also realises that God sees us with the eyes of absolute love: 'Your understanding of me brings me wonder and strength' (v. 6).

As a child I was told repeatedly that I shouldn't have been born. These words had a crippling effect, and I began to hate myself. I felt that I was a mistake. If you are struggling with such words today, God is saying to you, 'I saw who I created you to be even before you were born. Your life was written in my book. I knew your name and lovingly formed you myself to be uniquely wonderful. You were created not just by genes but by my plan.'

As David says: 'This is just too wonderful, deep and incomprehensible' (v. 6), but nevertheless, it is absolutely true.

When we suffer deep rejection, the enemy takes advantage, and it is vital that we resist his lies in the power of God's word. As the psalm draws to an end, we find the rather startling section where David cries out his hatred of God's enemies: 'Lord, can't you see how I despise those who despise you?' (v. 21). This makes me uncomfortable. What about love and forgiveness? I think what David is saying here is that we need to hate every destructive work of Satan and stand against it.

Knowing we are totally and unconditionally loved by God brings deep healing and peace. Let's follow David's example and take the time to reflect upon and drink in its truth.

O Lord, search my heart and examine me. Reach into the hidden places and expose those destructive lies. Free me from all anxiety and lead me on the path of truth that I am always held safe in your love. Amen.

TRACY WILLIAMSON

Healing dialogue

Why, my soul, are you downcast? Why so disturbed within me? Put your hope in God, for I will yet praise him, my Saviour and my God. (v. 5, NIV)

In this rich psalm we are invited to eavesdrop on the psalmist's personal conversations, both with God and with himself.

He begins by noticing a deer: 'As the deer pants for streams of water' (v. 1). His inner state is exposed as the deer's thirst makes him consider his own. Possibly he hasn't realised how dry he'd become, but noticing the thirsty deer opens an inward conversation. God will speak through the ordinary things around us; but while listening to him is so important, it's also vital to be in tune with our own hearts.

'When can I go and meet with God?' the psalmist asks (v. 2). Sometimes, when life is tough, all our energy becomes focused on coping. What does that tell us about what is happening inside? Have we lost our hope in God? From realising he is thirsty, the psalmist now finds himself remembering happier times. He is clearly grieving the loss of a loving and worshipful community. Taking the time to reflect on his thirst has brought to light a deeper need.

I find it hard to know my own heart. I may wake feeling sad but not know why. Reflective journalling can help to deepen our awareness of our inner voice. Writing your thoughts in a notebook or speaking into a recorder can help us to discover what is behind our feelings.

God is clearly guiding the psalmist's inner explorations: 'My soul is downcast within me; therefore I will remember you' (v. 6). He recalls the past magnitude of God's power and discovers afresh the constancy of his presence: 'By day the Lord directs his love, at night his song is with me' (v. 8). His faith is rising even though his situation is still crushing. His final words show the healing power of such reflection: 'I will yet praise him, my Saviour and my God' (v. 11).

Take a notebook and write: 'Lord, I feel…' Write down your thoughts, however random. Then try adding: 'Thank you, Father, for…' and jot down any ways that he's blessed you. Be enriched and encouraged in your journalling.

TRACY WILLIAMSON

Hear, O Israel

'Hear me, my people, and I will warn you – if you would only listen to me, Israel! You shall have no foreign god among you; you shall not worship any god other than me. I am the Lord your God, who brought you up out of Egypt.' (81:8–10, NIV)

These two psalms focus on the powerful God of all nations. With global TV and the internet, we are bombarded with world news, but do we pray and expect God to reveal his plans and his heart for the world?

Psalm 81 was written for a feast day and starts with celebration. We have many festivals too, celebrating music, diversity, food and creativity, but our specifically Christian festivals, which celebrate God, are buried under consumerism. These psalms reveal the importance of remembering God's character and ways. Asaph prophesies: 'In your distress you called and I rescued you' (81:7).

When we read God's heartfelt words: 'My people would not listen to me; Israel would not submit to me. So I gave them over to their stubborn hearts' (81:11–12), it's important to consider what that means for us today. They show the impact of rebellion within all nations. National rebellion means God will give us over to what we demand. I am part of that, and you are too. We see the effects everywhere with wars, displacements of entire people groups and trauma on a global scale.

God is always speaking and calling the nations to listen and know who he is. At the end of Psalm 82 Asaph prays: 'Rise up, O God, judge the earth, for all the nations are your inheritance' (v. 8). Will we use such psalms as these to search our own hearts and stand in prayer for the nations? Asaph prays that God will 'defend the weak and the fatherless' (82:3). How needed that prayer is in our world today. Will I be willing to be vulnerable and stand up and celebrate my God before unbelievers? Will I speak out for him? Will I pray? Most of all, will I listen and act?

Lord, I long to boldly stand up for you and declare your awesome ways. Forgive me for every time I've rebelled against you. Empower me for my nation's sake, to celebrate you, to pray and to act in your name. Amen.

TRACY WILLIAMSON

Delighting in the Lord

Oh, how I love your law! I meditate on it all day long… How sweet are your words to my taste, sweeter than honey to my mouth! I gain understanding from your precepts; therefore I hate every wrong path. Your word is a lamp for my feet. (vv. 97, 103–105, NIV)

I laughed at the prospect of using Psalm 119, but as I read, I felt deep joy. It is a treasure-filled psalm, with the writer declaring that he just can't live without God's word. Day and night he meditates on it, seeking God's guidance. Is it possible to have such a hunger for God and his word? We can feel condemned that we are not nearly as passionate, but God loves us unconditionally.

For me, the key question is in verse 9: 'How can a young person stay on the path of purity?' The psalmist answers: 'By living according to your word.' Whether we are already passionate about our faith or struggling with it, the key is living out what we read in God's word.

One of God's greatest laws is to forgive as he forgives us. As a young Christian, I knew that I was meant to forgive, but I hated this law because I wanted vengeance not forgiveness. One day my abusive stepfather hurt his finger during a violent rage. I gloated in his pain, but God's whisper came: 'Show that you love me: forgive him.' I struggled, but as I obeyed by staunching his blood, joy filled my heart and I felt released from his power.

The writer talks of meditating, delighting, rejoicing, following, recounting, praising and hiding God's word in his heart. Often, we hide our negative feelings more than God's word. We mull over that ugly retort or embarrassing situation, feeding on our distress until it consumes us. This psalm shows that God's way brings true healing: 'I remember… your ancient laws, and I find comfort in them' (v. 52).

I still have a long way to go, but if I ask God to help me live out even one verse of this amazing psalm each day, I know my life will be so enriched.

'Your word, Lord, is eternal; it stands firm in the heavens. Your faithfulness continues through all generations… Great peace have those who love your law, and nothing can make them stumble' (vv. 89–90, 165).

TRACY WILLIAMSON

Praise the Lord

Praise the Lord, my soul; all my inmost being, praise his holy name… forget not all his benefits – who forgives all your sins and heals all your diseases, who redeems your life from the pit and crowns you with love and compassion. (vv. 1–4, NIV)

I love this psalm because it focuses on the Lord's love and compassion. David exhorts his own soul to praise and tells his innermost being not to forget. We so easily remember the hurts but forget God's blessings and how much he loves us. So David urges himself to remember and to praise.

Talking to our inner selves is wonderfully liberating. Our soul and innermost being are our emotions, personalities and wills, and the enemy loves to attack us in those areas. David reminds himself that God forgives all his sins and later enlarges on this: 'As far as the east is from the west, so far has he removed our transgressions from us' (v. 12).

A man I was praying with was crippled by condemnation. My prayers seemed ineffective, but as I read these verses he leapt up, his crushed demeanour totally transformed. The power of God had released him from condemnation. He knew he was forgiven.

David remembers more benefits as he takes time to reflect on God's goodness. God reveals to him that he redeems our lives and crowns us with love and compassion. This promise has been deeply meaningful to me. My abusive childhood stole my dreams and made me want to hide, but God's plan was to restore me and resurrect those buried dreams. He covers our thoughts with the beauty and freedom of his love for us. In his compassion he carries our pain, crowning us with his joy and peace.

David shows that as we look back, we'll see God's hand on our lives. As we open our hearts to listen, the Holy Spirit will reveal beautiful things. Let's join with the angels in praising our wonderful God.

A message: Beloved, I have always known you and created you with joy to be unique and beautiful. I know your pain, but you are not the crushed daisy you think. Know that you are a rose full of beautiful colour and fragrance.

TRACY WILLIAMSON

The God who protects

Whoever dwells in the shelter of the Most High will rest in the shadow of the Almighty. I will say of the Lord, 'He is my refuge and my fortress, my God, in whom I trust'… You will not fear the terror of night, nor the arrow that flies by day. (vv. 1–2, 5, NIV)

Life is sometimes very scary. We make plans, but in a flash, something turns our world upside down. Despite our best efforts, we can't prevent those moments of bad news and their accompanying heartaches. How can we avoid anxiety, and what does it mean that Jesus is Lord if life is so fragile?

In this psalm the writer starts with the words 'Whoever dwells'. The key word here is 'dwell'. Jesus uses the same word in John 15:9: 'Now remain in my love.' It's about becoming established, not in a geographical location, but in God and in our trust in his love, power and protection.

When we dwell in God, we will find rest. This is referring to heart-rest or the gift of peace that Jesus promised us in John 14:27.

The psalm also teaches us that we need to speak out the truth of God's power to protect us. 'I will say of the Lord, "He is my refuge"' (v. 2). What we say is so important because it will either draw us under God's protection or open us up to attack from Satan.

When we dwell with God, we can face the things that may terrify others – serious illnesses, crippling life situations, wars or terrorist attacks – without fear. We know that Jesus has conquered death, and we can know his gift of security and peace. However, as the psalm indicates, this isn't a formula; rather, it must spring out of a love relationship with God: '"Because he loves me," says the Lord, "I will rescue him… He will call on me, and I will answer him"' (vv. 14–15).

When I become anxious, God whispers his promise that he is with me and calls me to be strong in his love. He whispers that to you too.

Father, I choose today to root myself deep in your love. Thank you for holding me and all I love safe under your wings. You are faithful and true, and I accept with joy your gift of peace. Amen.

TRACY WILLIAMSON.

The Lord's my shepherd

You prepare a table before me in the presence of my enemies. You have anointed *and* refreshed my head with oil… Surely goodness and mercy *and* unfailing love shall follow me all the days of my life, And I shall dwell forever… in the house *and* in the presence of the Lord. (vv. 5–6, AMP)

What better psalm to close this series than Psalm 23? We have journeyed from the disillusionment of Psalm 73 to bask in the certainty of God's promises in this well-loved psalm.

My first joy is how the young shepherd, David, hears the Lord speaking through his work. We've discussed listening to the Lord, and this is a beautiful example of how God can speak to us through the things we do in life.

David says, 'The Lord is my Shepherd' (v. 1). Somehow as he's walked the wilderness searching for pasture and water for his sheep, protected them from danger and guided them to right paths, God has spoken of how he is doing the very same for David and for us all. This makes me long to hear God bringing similar revelation through the ordinary things I do. If we expect him to, he will make himself known.

God gave David that joyful insight that he was constantly watching over him, to feed, guide, restore and protect him. Do you know that too?

David was often hunted by those intent on killing him. We too have an enemy who will do everything he can to destroy our faith. David discovered that even in the darkest times of loss and pain, God was there to comfort him. Today I believe someone reading this really needs to know this too. God is with you, there to comfort and help you; there to provide in amazing ways for you.

David ends with that wonderful promise of our eternal hope. Today at church I had a vision of us in heaven with Jesus. Jesus was full of glory, and yet we were all absolutely at home with him. Everyone belonged and there was joy, love, beauty, dancing, fun, worship and laughter. We were so at home with our shepherd, our king.

Lord, thank you for being my shepherd, constantly there to feed, guide and shield me. Thank you for your deep comfort in dark times and for the glorious promise that I will spend eternity at home with you, my beautiful king. Amen.

TRACY WILLIAMSON

God at home

Rachel Turner writes:

When we read scripture, we can easily note all the courageous, adventurous stories of the people of God: Paul's shipwreck, Peter's prison break, the battles of Joshua and the miraculous provision of manna for the Israelites. Normal life with God seems to be a never-ending series of exciting events: Jesus walks on water, Elijah sees God's fire come down from heaven and Jael kills an enemy general. The Bible seems full of stories about remarkable people doing huge things with God.

In comparison, our repetitive, small and unexciting lives can seem hard to fit into the biblical story of a faith-filled life. However, that belief is a lie that will rob us of one of the greatest gifts God has given us. The truth is that scripture is full of stories just like ours: gentle stories about who God is when he is at home with people he loves and how they encounter his presence, power and partnership in the midst of average days.

The core of our lives happens at home. It is the most intimate place, where we are the most vulnerable and authentic. My home is a mishmash of memories, personal treasures, self-expression and safety. It is where I can cry, be silly, wallow in old hobbies and try new things. It is a place I can choose to invite people into or shut myself away from the world.

I live with people in my home, so it is also a place of constant challenge and support, blessing and stress, where I need God's guidance and help. Our homes are at the centre of our lives, so of course, God will be there. An average day is where God loves to be because God's plan for us is to love him, love our neighbours and grow to be more like Jesus, producing fruit wherever we are planted.

Over the next two weeks, we will look at these biblical stories of who God is at home with us. We will explore how one of the most beautiful godly things we can do is be at home with God. Home is where he is inviting us to meet with him and to know him better, and it is where many of our greatest ministry opportunities are.

Home is where God is

Then they heard the Lord God walking in the garden during the cool part of the day. (3:8, NCV)

I grew up with a phrase that was said frequently: 'Home is where the heart is.' It was an encouragement to not cling to a particular house or location, but rather to see home as a place that can be cultivated wherever we go and choose to invest. In this passage, though, we see that the establishment of a home isn't limited to a building or emotional location. Home is where God is.

I have always loved the description of the garden of Eden: unspoilt nature, as it was created to be, and humans planted in the ideal location. What fascinates me most is how God interacted with the humans he created. He lovingly crafted them, spoke directly to them, brought the animals to them for naming and gave them purpose. When they sinned and heard him walking through the garden, they hid. They knew the sounds of his walk so well that in the midst of all nature, they could identify God's footfall. Their home was in the awareness and presence of God.

Today, our homes can sometimes feel the very opposite of that. Times of worry, deprivation or busyness can rob us of the idea of a home life with God. We can create a physical space within our four walls that makes us feel cosy and safe, relaxed and easy; but if we aren't also seeking to establish a home where we live in the awareness and presence of God, I think we will miss out on the purest experience of home. When God resides in our home, we feel true peace, deep love, contented joy and safety. Our home becomes a little slice of paradise.

God, I thank you that our home is in you. Make me aware of you as you live with me. Create your home in my home, that we may be together always. Amen.

RACHEL TURNER

God comes to find us in our homes

Simon's mother-in-law was sick in bed with a fever, and the people told Jesus about her. So Jesus went to her bed, took her hand, and helped her up. The fever left her, and she began serving them.
(vv. 30–31, NCV)

I hate being ill. Flu, cold, pneumonia, whatever it is, I am not one who can cough and carry on. I throw on my comfiest pyjamas, plop myself on the couch with a sick bowl or a massive packet of tissues and swaddle myself in blankets while I mindlessly watch old episodes of Agatha Christie's *Poirot*. I want to be private in my pain, unpresentable and miserable, unseen and unbothered.

Today's story is about a woman who was ill in bed. On one ordinary day, this woman had a high fever and chose to stay home from synagogue while her family and their friends went to the service. The gospel writers don't tell us the severity of the fever, but it didn't appear to be life-threatening or catastrophic. I can imagine her lying there, sweaty and miserable, and hearing the clatter of people returning to her home from synagogue while she snuggled in her bed.

At the time, people worked hard to get healing from Jesus. Wherever he went, a frenzy of people appeared, seeking him out to be healed. They came to find him wherever he was. This story is different, though.

Jesus came to her house to rest, eat and laugh with his friends. When he was told that she was ill, he got up and *came to find her*. He walked right into her bedroom, right into the place of her unpresentable vulnerability, sick and fevered as she was. And he healed her.

I love the idea of Jesus coming to find us in the hidden moments of our home life when we are sick and dishevelled, isolated from the world. When we are lonely in the prison of our not-quite-functioning bodies, God comes to us right where we are.

God, when I am ill, come close to me. When my body hurts and I want to retreat from the world, come right into my bedroom. Hold my hand in sickness, heal me and be with me. Amen.

RACHEL TURNER

Others can meet God in our homes

She and all the people in her house were baptised. Then she invited us to her home, saying, 'If you think I am truly a believer in the Lord, then come stay in my house.' And she persuaded us to stay with her. (v. 15, NCV)

The early church wasn't meeting in beautiful buildings or purpose-built gathering places. They met in ordinary homes, large and small, scattered across cities and rural areas. When Paul and his companions arrived in Philippi looking for a start, they ran into an open-hearted woman called Lydia. She responded to God and opened her home to host Paul and his friends. They lived with her and gathered believers in her home. It was the first church planted in Philippi.

Then Paul and Silas left, but the church in Lydia's home grew. It spread to other homes. More people came to know Jesus and share their lives together. Paul's letter of encouragement and teachings to believers who gathered in homes like Lydia's house in Philippi is recorded in the Bible as the book of Philippians. One woman, actively inviting people into her home, got to be an essential part of the church's growth.

Your home can be a place of nurturing faith and of welcome to those who want to know God more. You don't have to have a big, fancy or beautiful home. It doesn't have to be the best. It just needs to be open.

Our youth group didn't have a place to meet, so we had to stop our youth gatherings until an older couple in our church came to find me and told me they would love to open their home to us. Over the past year, so many teens got to ask questions about God, be prayed for, build friendships and study the Bible together because two people invited us in.

What could God do in and through you when you open your home to be a place of gathering and discipleship?

Ponder with God today about how you can open your home as a space for helping people meet and know God or gather together for encouragement and spiritual refreshment. Who is God poking your heart about?

RACHEL TURNER

We can host God in our homes

While Jesus and his followers were travelling, Jesus went into a town. A woman named Martha let Jesus stay at her house. (v. 38, NCV)

Have you ever been wonderfully hosted in someone's home? What is your best experience? What made it so welcoming?

I am writing this in Australia, in the guest room of someone's home. Whenever I am hosted in someone's home, I am deeply grateful. After a day of long travelling or exhausting speaking, I can arrive at a place of safety and care where I can be myself and have my needs considered. I am so aware that I have been welcomed into their personal space, their ordinary, everyday place of joy, safety, struggle and creativity. It is a privilege to be hosted.

Mary and Martha hosted Jesus. He could rock up with his friends, and Mary and Martha would open their home and welcome them in. Jesus made himself at home in their home. He often visited to retreat, relax and be with the people he loved.

Can we still host Jesus? What would it look like to consider ourselves hosts to Jesus in our homes, welcoming him in to make himself at home in our home? So often we seek God with an agenda, a thing we want him to do for us. What if we invited him to be with us in our homes, welcome at our tables, sit with us as we read and be a companion in our days? One of my favourite things to do with Jesus is to invite him to watch TV with me. What does it look like for you to invite Jesus into your home?

Jesus, make yourself at home in our home. Move into our everyday spaces and sit with us and laugh with us. Help us turn our hearts towards enjoying and hosting you as we live together at home. Amen.

RACHEL TURNER

Traditions connect us with God in our homes

There are six days for you to work, but the seventh day will be a special day of rest. It is a day for a holy meeting; you must not do any work. It is a Sabbath to the Lord in all your homes. (v. 3, NCV)

What is your favourite holiday? For sheer colour, food and music, I adore Christmas. I'm the scary, over-the-top friend who always wears a Christmas hat, plays Christmas music exclusively throughout December and force-feeds everyone festive goodies.

I love how God created humans to love celebrations in ordinary life. Part of God's law in the Old Testament commands his people to have traditions at home that reminded them of God and what he had done. Some of these traditions involved living outside in temporary shelters (like camping) to remind them of how God led them in the wilderness, blowing trumpets to declare a new season and eating a type of bread to remind them of leaving Egypt. Rituals and traditions can be a powerful tool in our homes to remind ourselves of God's character and history with us in our everyday lives.

After my total hysterectomy that removed my cancer, I was given access to HRT (hormone replacement therapy) through a little patch that I put on my leg. I replace it twice a week, but there is always some sticky residue from the glue. I wanted to establish a tradition of gratefulness around my memory of cancer, so I bought some beautiful smelling oil in a gorgeous jar. When I remove my HRT patch, I rub this oil on the spot to remove the residue, and I thank God for the gift of my life and for who he was for me amid my cancer season. This tiny ritual I do twice a week instantly anchors my heart in gratefulness to God and peace about the present.

What do you need to be reminded of this season, and what rituals or traditions in your home can you establish to help?

Discuss with God about what traditions or rituals you might want to try in your home to anchor you in who God is and what he has done in your life. Let God remind you and inspire you!

RACHEL TURNER

God provides the daily bread for our homes

The woman and her son and Elijah had enough food every day. The jar of flour and the jug of oil were never empty, just as the Lord, through Elijah, had promised. (vv. 15–16, NCV)

The first time I realised that we did not have enough money for food was early on in our marriage. I was home, bedridden with a chronic illness, and my husband had been searching for work after being made redundant. We were almost out of food and there was no money in the bank account. I felt helpless and afraid.

The widow in this passage had it much worse. She had a child to care for and only one small meal left. She had no hope for the future. There was no pathway to rescue. She had accepted that she and her child were going to die.

Our homes are where our most basic needs are expected to be met. Throughout scripture, God demonstrates that he concerns himself with the necessities of home. He gave manna to the Israelites while they were in the wilderness, and for this desperate single mother, he ensured that her jars of supplies never ran out. He provided their daily bread.

Jesus encouraged the disciples to ask God for their needs when he showed them how to pray: 'Give us this day our daily bread' (Matthew 6:11, NKJV). Bringing our ordinary, everyday needs to God is part of life with God at home. He wants us to ask, and he wants us to expect that he will provide. We have a God who loves us and cares about the basic needs of a household. We are not forgotten or unseen.

When we had no food, I regularly found a bag of groceries outside my front door, dropped off by God's people. They would leave notes saying that God brought us to mind when they were shopping. Our daily bread was provided by the God who cared. What do you need from God today?

God, I ask you to provide for my basic needs today. Make me open to being nudged by you to be your hands and feet to provide for other's basic needs too. Show me where to give. Amen.

RACHEL TURNER

God interrupts us at home

Mary said, 'I am the servant of the Lord. Let this happen to me as you say!' Then the angel went away. (v. 38, NCV)

Women's lives in the first century AD were full of chores. From sunrise to sunset, there were jobs to do: laundry, cooking, gardening, gathering water. The work of the home was constant. I've always wondered what Mary was doing when the angel interrupted her. I'm sure it was one of the endless ordinary tasks on the large list. An ordinary day at home which was interrupted by the God of the universe, and she was ready to respond.

God seems to like to talk to people in the middle of their ordinaries. Joshua, Gideon and Matthew are a few, and I'm sure Jesus interrupted Mary all the time as a child! It is so easy for us to have no expectations of God when ploughing through our home tasks. We can mindlessly whip through the dishes, changing sheets and hoovering without a thought about God or that he might want to engage with us. How would our days look different if we expected God to interrupt us?

One day I was folding laundry on the couch while watching a documentary. In the back of my mind, I was half thinking about some emotional struggles I was having with our current family situation. I hadn't prayed about it yet or even wanted to acknowledge those emotions, but it was playing on my mind. Suddenly, a thought popped up in my head. 'So, how about we talk about it now?' I paused my folding. Then I paused the TV. Over the years, I've learned to recognise when and how God communicates with me. I took a deep breath and considered telling him 'No.' Then I burst into tears.

Months of built-up stress, worries and thoughts came out as I cried on the couch, covered in half-sorted piles of laundry. When I picked up the job again, I had a solution and a sense of peace.

When we are interruptible in our daily chores and ready to respond, we are open to what God wants to do today.

God, I am up for your interruptions! Make me aware of you as I go about my ordinary tasks. Talk with me, remind me of you and place opportunities in front of me to do things with you. Amen.

RACHEL TURNER

My home can be a small part of someone else's grand story

'Go to the house of Judas on Straight Street and ask for a man from Tarsus named Saul, for he is praying.' (v. 11, NIV)

I am fascinated with minor characters in the Bible: people who lived full, interesting lives, but we only hear about them in a sentence or two. I can't help when I read this story to think about Judas.

At that time, Saul was a terrifying hunter of Christians. He was headed to Damascus to uncover, arrest and transport Christians to Jerusalem. Then he encountered Jesus on the road and was blinded and shaken. His companions led him by the hand to Judas' house, where he stayed for three days waiting. Was he always going to stay at Judas' house? If so, was Judas a fellow Jew with similar feelings about Christians?

All we know about Judas is that he lived on Straight Street and hosted Saul. I'm sure Judas just expected to give hospitality and wave his visitor on his way. Instead, Saul had one of the most significant moments of his life in Judas' home. Judas saw a Pharisee reborn in faith and a physical miracle happened in front of his eyes. Right in his home.

I have stayed in many people's homes: friends, relatives, hosts when I travel. I have often had conversations that helped me spiritually, heard things that inspired me, had people pray for me and had significant conversations with God overnight. In the little sanctuary of their homes, I was changed. I never told most of them, but I left different than when I arrived.

You will never truly know the impact you and your home can have on the people you host, but you can be sure that God will be at work in your home. When you have guests, ask God: 'What are you doing in their lives, and how can I serve what you are doing?'

God, use my home for your purposes. Bring people here and meet with them in significant ways. Amen.

RACHEL TURNER

Yes! And...

[Apollos] **had been instructed in the way of the Lord, and he spoke with great fervour and taught about Jesus accurately, though he knew only the baptism of John... When Priscilla and Aquila heard him, they invited him to their home and explained to him the way of God more adequately. (vv. 25–26, NIV)**

Some of my favourite memories from childhood were our weekly lunches with people from church. We would eat and talk at our house, their house or occasionally at a restaurant. We would debrief the sermon or share about what God was doing in our lives. I loved feeling equal and listened to; it was amazing to hear their stories and thoughts.

The people we would eat with always made me feel a huge 'Yes!' when I talked about God or the church. They would often add their own 'And...' to what I had to say, sharing their experiences of what I talked about, showing me other parts of the Bible that supported what I had to say, or adding in a complexity that made me think. This beautiful 'Yes! And...' pattern was so validating and stretching for me, and I did the same for them.

In today's reading, we see a young, excited preacher called Apollos, a capable and passionate speaker. Priscilla and Aquila invite him into their home and have one of those beautiful 'Yes! And...' conversations with him. They share their stories and knowledge that supported and added to his knowledge. They choose to pull him close, bring him into their home, and be a wonderful community around him. He becomes a significant church leader, helped by two people who invited him home from church.

You have wisdom and stories to share. There will be people to invite into your home and have wonderful 'Yes! And...' conversations with – not to correct or argue with but to add to their knowledge and confidence. Tell your stories, share scripture, listen well and sweep up those who could use a powerful 'Yes! And...'

God, highlight to me people at church or in my community who need some-one to welcome them home and have vibrant 'Yes! And...' conversations with. Who needs that kind of encouragement and help, Lord? Amen.

RACHEL TURNER

Ministering to the Lord in your home

I tell you that her many sins are forgiven, so she showed great love. But the person who is forgiven only a little will love only a little.
(v. 47, NCV)

Many of the worship leaders in the Old Testament considered it their job to minister *to* God, singing to him, loving him, praising him and blessing him. I always found it an odd idea. Why would God want a human to just be sitting in front of him, telling him how great he is all the time? Kind of egotistical, isn't it? Then I remembered this story of a woman who was so grateful to Jesus that she felt she had to come and minister to him. She crashed a dinner party in a Pharisee's home to try to care for him, showing her thanks and joy.

I remember other stories too. How Mary and Martha hosted Jesus in their home and poured their love into feeding him and giving him a place of rest. How David enjoyed God in nature on the hills where he lived, talking to him and making poems and songs to please him. Not once did Jesus or Father God demand for them to do this. Their ministering to God was an overflow of love to a God who loved them back.

I was intrigued by the idea of making my home a place to minister to God. What would change in my approach to life with God if I was focused on ministering *to* him rather than on what he can bring to me? I wanted my home to be a place of honesty with God, where he felt blessed by me as I felt blessed by him. I began to sing more worship songs around the house and randomly express, 'Oh God, I love how you make clouds!' when looking out the window, and I took my time in the shower to tell him how wonderful I thought he was.

My home felt more joyful, and my days more connected to God, just by choosing to minister to him.

Take a few moments to pause and take a few breaths. Then, tell God three reasons why you are grateful for him. Keep going if you want to do more.

RACHEL TURNER

Ministry at home can be messy

Since they could not get to Jesus because of the crowd, they dug a hole in the roof above where he was speaking. When they got through, they lowered the mat with the paralysed man on it. (v. 4, NCV)

Can you imagine this scenario? A guest speaker at church comes to your house for lunch, followed by a huge crowd all trying to get in. It is heaving in your home, and you see more people outside. Then suddenly, you hear a scraping, thumping sound and the plaster from your ceiling begins to crumble and fall. You look up to see your ceiling caving in as people rip it open to get to the guest speaker.

This is the scenario in our passage. In the Bible story, a beautiful and powerful miracle happens next. Jesus forgives a man's sin and heals his body. It is electrifying to the crowd! At some point, Jesus heads for the lake and the crowd follow him, leaving one house owner with a huge hole in the roof and a messed-up home. Sometimes, ministry can be messy.

There can be a cost to opening your home: people will sit in places you don't want, cups will be spilt and dishes may get broken. Before people come over to our flat, we have the panic tidy, and when they leave, I am picking up crumbs and finding mugs all over the place. There is a cost. Acknowledging and accepting it as part of the ministry is important.

However, it is so worth it. People meet with Jesus, get loved by a community, are encouraged in their faith, find friends, feel a purpose, connect with a new family and contribute to the faith lives of others. God brings enormous fruit when we open our homes.

When I think of the family with the hole in the roof, I imagine they looked at the mess and were reminded of the beautiful thing Jesus did in their home – a small price to pay for something so great.

God, fill me with peace about my home. Use my home as you want. I accept the mess and let go of control. Do wonderful things in my home for people who need you. Amen.

RACHEL TURNER

Wisdom in the home

Naaman's servants came near and said to him, 'My father, if the prophet had told you to do some great thing, wouldn't you have done it? Doesn't it make more sense just to do it? After all, he only told you, "Wash, and you will be clean."' (v. 13, NCV)

One of the greatest gifts God has given us is the people who are woven into our everyday lives: roommates, friends we invite round, family or care workers. When we face the big questions in life, it can be very easy to look for solutions in books or media from experts or pastors.

In this story, we see God working through something far closer to home – the people in it. For Naaman, it was an enslaved girl and his household staff. They were people with no significant qualifications or expertise. They were simply there and confident enough to counsel him, and he was wise enough to listen. It's a remarkable story of an army commander who repeatedly takes the advice and direction of those who live with him.

I live with my husband and my son, and there have been many occasions when I have sensed God's guidance and wisdom through their words. We chose the church we attend because my six-year-old explained why we needed them and why they needed us. As he spoke, my husband and I felt God's truth, so we joined the church. When I was struggling to decide about my job, my husband referred me to a Bible story that confirmed what God had been stirring in my heart about the situation.

Having people around us who know and love God is a tremendous gift. God wants to communicate with you right where you are, directly to you, but also be open to his wisdom and guidance through the people living closest to you. No one is too young to be used by God or too insignificant to be helpful.

God, open my heart and mind to your communications that come through people in my home. Give me discernment to find your truth and wisdom, expecting it to come through young and old. Amen.

RACHEL TURNER

Home away from home

This is what the Lord All-Powerful, the God of Israel, says to all those people I sent away from Jerusalem as captives to Babylon: 'Build houses and settle in the land. Plant gardens and eat the food they grow.' (vv. 4–5, NCV)

I sat in my lounge in the evening, trying to read a book while the thin wall next to me pounded with the beat of the music from the raucous party next door. 'God, what are we doing here?!', I prayed as profanity drifted through my windows from people smoking outside. I was in an oppressive job, in a town I struggled to love, in a house where we never had peace. 'This can never feel like home to me!' I told God, 'And you sent us here!'

The Israelites had a season where they were far from home, too. They had forgotten how to live with God, so after many warnings, he allowed an enemy to capture the people and take them far from the homes he had given them. It wasn't where they wanted to be, but it was where they needed to be to learn what they needed to learn.

God assured them that he would restore them to their land in 70 years, and he gave them instructions for the season of being away from home. He told them to invest in where they were, grab on to where they found themselves and establish a life. They were to work and pray for the good of the place they found themselves in, and to trust in the goodness and faithfulness of God.

God reminded me of this truth that evening I was in despair. We invested in our neighbours and saw God do significant things in both our lives and theirs. It was still loud, but simply by choosing to claim the place we were as home, it became a place of purpose and joy. It wasn't quiet, but it was fruitful.

God, help me create a home when I feel out of place and far from where I want to be. Open my eyes to others who feel like they are in exile and are struggling to feel at home. Amen.

RACHEL TURNER

Forever home

'There are many rooms in my Father's house; I would not tell you this if it were not true. I am going there to prepare a place for you.' (v. 2, NCV)

Home is where God is. In our homes, we can find a deep connection with God as we host and minister to him. It is a place where he will sit with us and provide for us. He will meet with us when we are busy doing chores, when we are ill or in our traditions. If we open our homes, he will use them as powerful places of ministry to others. People will meet God in our homes, find family and discipleship. They will grow in their faith, and we will be a small part of their grand life journey with God. We can create a home of peace and purpose with God wherever our house is.

However, there is a better home coming – one beyond what we can even imagine here on earth. Jesus wanted to ensure that his followers knew that they would enter a forever home after death – a home of his design, where they would live with God forever. It will be a home where there will be no tears or death, and everything will be made new (Revelation 21:1–4). This forever home is ahead of us. One day, we will all die, but for those who choose life in Jesus, a home with him for eternity is guaranteed.

One evening, while in hospital after my cancer operation, I heard a fellow patient crying. We whispered for a few hours, talking about the uncertainty of the treatment and what might happen if our cancer turned out to be terminal. She was terrified of death and the nothingness that she felt was on the other side, whereas I knew without a doubt that death would simply be a door to my new home – a wonderful one that Jesus has prepared for all who say yes to him.

Thank you, God, that our current homes are not our forever homes. Thank you for the hope of a future life with you. Make our current homes a dim reflection of the glory of our future home. Amen.

RACHEL TURNER

John, the patron saint of Advent

Emma Scrivener writes:

If Advent had a soundtrack, it would be that haunting carol 'O come, O come Emmanuel' because it's all about waiting for Christ – straining ahead with breathless anticipation for the long-awaited Messiah.

If Advent had a patron saint, it would be John the Baptist. He appears in the New Testament, but he is often considered to be the last of the Old Testament prophets, and his message is the summary of theirs. He is 'A voice of one calling: "In the wilderness prepare the way for the Lord"' (Isaiah 40:3, NIV). John is like Advent personified, preparing us for the coming Christ.

My favourite depiction of John is from a painting by Matthias Grünewald (1470–1528). He is shown at the crucifixion of Jesus. In real life John was beheaded before Jesus died, but the painting is rich in symbolism. You get a true sense of John when you see him next to his Saviour. He stands at the foot of the cross holding the Old Testament in one hand and pointing to Christ with the other – with the longest finger you've ever seen. Next to him are the words of John 3:30 (NKJV): 'He must increase, but I *must* decrease.'

That's John: a witness. He's the witness to Jesus in the Bible. His whole life is like that finger, pointing to 'the Lamb of God, who takes away the sin of the world!' (John 1:29, NIV). This means that as we study John over the next seven days, we will be taken in two directions.

On the one hand we will be confronted by the most dazzling example of a follower of Christ. As Jesus said, 'John was a lamp that burned and gave light' (John 5:35, NIV). Have you ever said of someone, 'They're on fire for Jesus'? Well, that's what Jesus says about John! As a blazing witness to Christ, John will challenge us all. That's because as we follow Jesus, we are called to be witnesses too (Acts 1:8).

On the other hand, John is not simply an example for us to follow. Our eyes should not remain on him. We need to follow that pointing finger all the way to Jesus. So, this week, let's pray that, like John, we will also 'behold the Lamb'.

Leap for joy

When Elizabeth heard Mary's greeting, the baby [John the Baptist] leaped in her womb, and Elizabeth was filled with the Holy Spirit. (v. 41, NIV)

The coming of John was prophesied three times in the Old Testament (Isaiah 40:1–3; Malachi 3:1; 4:5). He began testifying to Christ before the very first Christmas – in fact, before his own birth! In this sense, John is the last of the Old Testament prophets. As Jesus said, 'For all the Prophets and the Law prophesied until John. And if you are willing to accept it, he is the Elijah who was to come' (Matthew 11:13–14). The Old Testament predicted a prophet who would be like Elijah. In other words, someone anointed by the Lord to preach repentance to the people and salvation in his name. That's John's job description – and he starts work before he's even left the womb.

Even in his mother's tummy, John leaps to be near Jesus. What a prophet! He's not even been born and already he's preaching to his mum. John's excitement at the presence of Jesus is infectious; and as her child moves, Elizabeth is filled with the Holy Spirit. So, John is introduced to us as someone who is utterly sold out for Jesus. From before birth through to his death, he is captivated by the Lord, which leads us to ask: what was Jesus like?

The Bible tells us that John came to prepare the way of the Lord (Isaiah 40:3). In the original Hebrew, 'Lord' describes the sacred name of 'Yahweh'. This is like God saying, 'The God who always was and is and will be.' That's who Jesus is, right from the womb. Notice that Elizabeth calls Mary 'the mother of my Lord' (Luke 1:43). John might be an exalted prophet, but Jesus is the great I am, the maker of heaven and earth, the Lord!

In a deep sense, the wonder is not that John leapt for joy, it's how anyone wouldn't.

Lord, thank you for your word and for your servant John. May we share John's excitement and wonder at the Lord who came for us. May we rejoice in Jesus today and recognise his nearness to us. Amen.

EMMA SCRIVENER

Go against the grain

And the child grew and became strong in spirit; and he lived in the wilderness until he appeared publicly to Israel. (v. 80, NIV)

It's hard to go against the grain, isn't it? We want to fit in and to be accepted. Life can be tough enough without courting controversy; but what if, as believers, we're called to something else?

John the Baptist knew what it meant to stand out from the crowd. As an adult he famously lived on a diet of honey and locusts – desert food (Matthew 3:4) – but, as our reading today makes clear, John was a desert-dweller from the beginning, and after his birth he was dedicated as a Nazirite (Luke 1:15). This meant that he had to follow certain rules about holiness, like not cutting his hair, not drinking alcohol and avoiding contact with dead bodies and graves. His was a life of self-denial and service and, despite mockery and rejection, he wasn't afraid to be different. In fact, he 'grew and became strong in spirit'.

How did he do this? The gospel he proclaimed was central. His whole message was 'to give his people the knowledge of salvation through the forgiveness of their sins, because of the tender mercy of our God' (1:77).

As witnesses to Jesus, we are called to something similar. We proclaim a gospel that is sometimes despised. We do this not to be difficult, but because we want to give people 'knowledge of salvation'. We stand against sin not because we're moralists but because we believe in 'the forgiveness of their sins'. At times we embrace the wilderness, not because we want to be stoics, but because this is where we can meet 'the tender mercy of our God'.

We may find ourselves going against the grain of the world but, from God's perspective, we're travelling 'the path of peace' (1:79).

Father, help us to endure with grace whatever rejection or difficulty your gospel demands and to know all the comforts and blessings your Son provides. Guide our feet in the path of his peace, in Jesus' name. Amen.

EMMA SCRIVENER

Turn around!

'I baptise you with water. But one who is more powerful than I will come, the straps of whose sandals I am not worthy to untie. He will baptise you with the Holy Spirit and fire.' (v. 16, NIV)

John the Baptist preached to both princes and paupers, but his message always remained the same: *A king is coming, and he changes everything*. 'Every valley shall be filled in, every mountain and hill made low' (v. 5).

In the Bible, mountains are associated with kingdoms, while valleys represent difficulties (think of 'the valley of the shadow of death' in Psalm 23). John testifies that the coming king (Jesus) will bring down the lofty and raise up the lowly. Whether high or humble, those who come to his kingdom must all accept the same thing: a baptism of repentance.

A baptism is a wash, and 'repentance' means turning around. The people queued to be washed by John, so that they could start again with Jesus. This makes what happens next even more surprising. Incredibly, Jesus himself comes to the River Jordan and is baptised by John. Jesus joins all the messy, sinful people in the waters – not because he *is* a sinner but because he is *for* sinners. He is the high and lofty one who joins us in the valley of our humanity. He keeps on descending, all the way to the cross where he becomes our sin (2 Corinthians 5:21). Then, he can lift us from our valley and raise us to his heights.

It's a wonderful gospel. No wonder 'John exhorted the people and proclaimed the good news to them' (Luke 3:18). John's baptisms didn't save people, but the gospel he preached did. John could only make people wet, but Jesus gives the true baptism (3:16). He endured our sin on the cross, to give us his Spirit. So today, let's once again repent and believe the good news.

Jesus, I bring before you all that's high and lifted up – my pride and sin – and I turn from it. I bring before you all that's poor and lowly – my needs and weakness – and I seek your Spirit's help. Amen.

EMMA SCRIVENER

Behold the Lamb

The next day John saw Jesus coming towards him and said, 'Look, the Lamb of God, who takes away the sin of the world!' (v. 29, NIV)

John is famous for baptising people, but it's his preaching that continues to impact the world. The heart of his message is this: *Look at Jesus, the Lamb of God.*

John could have described Jesus as 'the word of God', 'the Christ of God', 'the priest of God' or a thousand other titles. But, according to John, our first need is to encounter Jesus as our Lamb. Why?

Rewind to 2,000 BC. Abraham is trudging up a hill near modern-day Jerusalem with his beloved son, Isaac. Isaac asks: 'Father... where is the lamb for the burnt offering?' (Genesis 22:7). Abraham replies: 'God himself will provide the lamb' (v. 8). As we read on in Genesis 22, we discover that the Lord provides a ram for the burnt offering and from then on, the mountain is called 'The Lord Will Provide" (Genesis 22:14). The Lamb will be given on this mountain in the region of Jerusalem!

Fast forward 500 years. It's Passover, and the Lord provides a different kind of lamb. This one will die in the place of the eldest son of the household, and its blood will be painted on the door frame with hyssop. The lamb saves.

Fast forward another 500 years, and David is begging the Lord for forgiveness. 'Cleanse me with hyssop and I shall be clean,' he prays in Psalm 51. God has hyssop, but does he have a lamb?

Fast forward yet another 500 years and Isaiah is foretelling the coming of Christ. He would be led 'like a lamb to the slaughter' to bring us peace (Isaiah 53:7).

When John sees Jesus, it is the fulfilment of the ages. With Jesus we have God's provision, salvation, forgiveness and peace. He is the sacrifice for the sins of the whole world. In response we are called to 'look'!

Father, help us to see Jesus with the eyes of faith. May we know the wonders of his sacrificial love ever more deeply. Amen.

EMMA SCRIVENER

The humility of John

'The friend who attends the bridegroom… is full of joy when he hears the bridegroom's voice. That joy is mine, and it is now complete. He must become greater; I must become less.' (3:29–30, NIV)

Jesus described John the Baptist as 'a lamp that burned and gave light' (John 5:35). He was a dazzling witness to Christ. That's important to know because we too are called to witness to Jesus (Acts 1:8). We are commanded not to put our light under a bowl (Matthew 5:14–15). So how can we learn from John?

John shone, but not by drawing attention to his many achievements. He might have been the most naturally gifted man ever to walk the planet – that seems to have been Jesus' view anyway (Matthew 11:11) – but instead of pointing to himself, John pointed to Christ.

'He himself was not the light,' as John 1:8 tells us, 'he came only as a witness to the light.' John testified to the truth (John 5:33). He was always pointing beyond himself and towards Jesus.

We're all meant to shine, but John shows us how. We're all witnesses, but John is the ultimate example. John teaches us to think of ourselves in relation to Jesus. Like a best man on the groom's wedding day, we know it's not about us. We are just filled with joy to be his friend and so, happily, we point to him. We shine the most when we simply turn to the true light of the world. May his self-appraisal be ours:

- 'I am not the Messiah' (John 1:20).
- 'I am the voice of one calling in the wilderness, "Make straight the way for the Lord"' (John 1:23).
- 'He is the one who comes after me, the straps of whose sandals I am not worthy to untie' (John 1:27).
- 'He must become greater; I must become less' (John 3:30).

Jesus, help me to hear your voice and fill me with your joy. May I gladly point to you all my days. Amen.

EMMA SCRIVENER

The doubts of John

When John, who was in prison, heard about the deeds of the Messiah, he sent his disciples to ask him, 'Are you the one who is to come, or should we expect someone else?' (vv. 2–3, NIV)

Even John had doubts and we can understand why. He's locked up in a first-century prison and it will prove to be death row for him. He has proclaimed a gospel in which the Lord raises up every valley and brings down every lofty mountain (Luke 3:5). Surely that means John should be lifted from this pit, and Herod (who has imprisoned him) should be brought low? Sadly not. Herod remains on top, and John is left to rot at the bottom of a dungeon. Perhaps John had it all wrong – maybe Jesus wasn't the Lord he thought he was.

Imagine John alone in his cell, asking himself, 'Have I trusted in the wrong person?' It's very human!

We too have questions. Perhaps we see the wicked on top and the righteous suffering. Perhaps we look at Jesus and wonder, 'Is he really the one?'

If that's us today, then we need to see how Jesus responds to John. Jesus encouraged John to do the opposite of what he's been doing. John has been reading the scriptures through the lens of his life circumstances. Jesus tells him to read his life circumstances through the lens of the scriptures: 'The blind receive sight, the lame walk, those who have leprosy are cleansed, the deaf hear, the dead are raised, and the good news is proclaimed to the poor' (v. 5).

In effect he's saying, 'Who else has ever fulfilled the prophecies of Isaiah 35 (and all the rest!)? Who else could you be waiting for, except me?'

These are questions for us too. Right now, we may be in a pit or filled with doubts. Yet Jesus has fulfilled the scriptures and changed eternal history. No one is more powerful, more loving or more trustworthy than him. So, when our hearts and feelings start to wobble, let's follow John's lead and bring them to Jesus.

Lord Jesus, I am often in a pit, and I don't know what you're doing. Help me to see you, and to see my life and my doubts in the light of your word and your truth. Amen.

EMMA SCRIVENER

The death of John

John had been saying to Herod, 'It is not lawful for you to have your brother's wife'… When Herod heard John, he was greatly puzzled; yet he liked to listen to him. (vv. 18, 20, NIV)

Jesus said, 'The truth will set you free' (John 8:32). If that's true, how do we make sense of John the Baptist's death? John preached the truth about King Herod's unlawful marriage, and yet he was thrown in prison! Something much deeper was going on.

Herod had a complicated relationship with the truth. He liked to hear John preach but he never acted on it. His wife, on the other hand, was more decisive. She started plotting to kill John (v. 19) and at Herod's birthday feast, she saw her opportunity. While the king and guests were drunk, she sent her daughter to dance for the court. Foolishly, Herod promised to give her anything she asked for (vv. 21–23). With one careless oath, John's fate was sealed. Having consulted with her mother, the girl asks for the head of John the Baptist on a platter (v. 25). It is done. John was sentenced to death, and Herod cut off the head of the one person who dared to tell him the truth.

So, does the truth really set us free? Yes! It could have liberated Herod, if only he had listened. It could have released him from his besetting sin and brought him to God. And, in a strange way, the truth *did* set John free. In his martyrdom, he completed a life of witness — a life lived pointing to Jesus. He died for truth but lives now in an eternal kingdom and is famous across the globe. Herod, however, is a petty, largely vilified man. The truth came knocking and he refused to answer. So, when it comes to truth, will we stand with Herod or with John?

Psalm 95:7–8 puts our challenge most plainly: 'Today, if only you would hear his voice, "Do not harden your hearts."'

Father, today may we hear your voice, may we not harden our hearts and may your truth set us free. In Jesus' name, Amen.

EMMA SCRIVENER

Intimacy with God

Sheila Jacobs writes:

Many of us will be familiar with this verse from Jeremiah 29: '"For I know the plans I have for you," declares the Lord, "plans to prosper you and not to harm you, plans to give you hope and a future"' (v. 11, NIV); but do we then read on further? Verse 13 tells us: 'You will seek me and find me when you seek me with all your heart.' Seeking him wholeheartedly has a great reward – real intimacy with the living God, who loves us more than we can fully understand.

Can we really have that true, intimate encounter, that satisfying and rewarding relationship with our creator? Yes, we can.

The Christian life is not a set of religious rules to follow. It's about the one who loves us so much that he sent his only Son so that we could have a restored relationship with him. That restoration means we won't be separated from him for eternity. More than that, we can walk with him, knowing his companionship throughout our lives here on earth.

Intimacy with anyone involves vulnerability. It's about knowing someone and being known. God made himself vulnerable in the form of a child, born in a stable, and he knew what it was to be tired and thirsty, to weep and to know joy. Jesus is the human face of God, and his disciples were able to know him. We too can know him, as we turn to him and allow him to fill us with his Holy Spirit, who lives with us and in us and will reveal Jesus to us. We are also invited to make ourselves vulnerable, to surrender in trust to the one who loves us and longs to heal, revive and restore us.

There are some verses in John's gospel (1:37–39) that are easy to miss, but they speak of the intimacy the first followers had with Jesus. He asks them, 'What do you want?' They answer, in effect, that they want to get to know him better; then they spend time with him. It's challenging to think about how we might answer that same question.

I love being with friends, but any friendship involves interaction, connection and listening as well as speaking, getting to know what makes that person 'tick'. I pray these notes encourage you to want to spend more time with the one who invites you into close, personal relationship with him. Let's seek him together!

Hiding

Then the man and his wife heard the sound of the Lord God as he was walking in the garden in the cool of the day, and they hid from the Lord God… But the Lord God called to the man, 'Where are you?' (vv. 8–9, NIV)

It all starts here. The first man and the first woman were enjoying friendship with God, walking with him in the garden, discussing the plants, the animals and trees, and whatever else was on their minds as they discovered more and more about their earthly paradise. What would it have been like walking with God, sharing thoughts and feelings in openness with him and with each other?

Unfortunately, it all went horribly wrong. Adam and Eve disobeyed God, and instead of freedom and excitement, they found fear and bondage. They hid from the one who had created them for love and fellowship with himself.

Fear does that; it makes us want to run. When we know we're not right with God, when we've done or are doing something that we know isn't part of his good plan for our lives, we hide away from him. We try to cover our faults and failings and our shame and block our ears to his tender call: 'Come back. Talk to me. Let me into that place of pain and failure. Let me restore you.'

In Psalm 23, David talks about the restoration and refreshing of our soul, as we sit quietly with God. We need to stop running or hiding and 'be still, and know that [he is] God' (Psalm 46:10) if we want to know true intimacy with him.

Perhaps you don't feel 'right' with God today. Stop! Don't strive. Let him find you. Begin your journey of fresh intimacy with him.

God wants us to know his friendship and to walk with him, but to walk with God we need to start with a pause. Take a breath. Turn around. Don't hide.

Lord, I really want to walk more closely with you. I don't want to hide anymore. Help me to step out into your presence and come close to you. I know you will come close to me. Amen.

SHEILA JACOBS

Friends

Whenever the people saw the pillar of cloud standing at the entrance to the tent, they all stood and worshipped, each at the entrance to their tent. The Lord would speak to Moses face to face, as one speaks to a friend. (vv. 10–11, NIV)

I am very blessed to have some good friends – some I've known since early adulthood; others I have befriended along the way. These are people who accept me, who love me and who may very well correct me when they see something they believe needs addressing! Because I know they care for me, I trust them. There's a knowing, a fond acceptance with a good friend that is precious beyond words. I also have friends from further back, people from my childhood who I don't see regularly but who are still important to me. Perhaps you do, too.

It's amazing to read that God spoke to Moses 'as one speaks to a friend' (v. 11). Moses knows he has found favour with God and that God is pleased with him. What a lovely, relaxed relationship we see here. I love the conversation in this passage: 'I'll come with you on your journey,' says the Lord, and Moses effectively responds, 'Well, if you don't, I'm not going anywhere!' The presence of God is vital to Moses. Why would he want to step out of it?

Have you known the presence of God – the drawing close of the peaceful presence that brings rest and restoration? To live in that presence is to know true intimacy with him.

When we're getting along well with friends, it brings joy, comfort and laughter. We want to be with them and spend time with them, but we need to invest in that relationship. Keeping in contact isn't always easy because of our busy lives, but we tend to make space for the things we really want to do in life – and the people we want to keep in touch with.

If we want true intimacy with God, it's available. So – do we want it?

What might stop you walking into true intimacy and close friendship with God? Think and pray about it.

SHEILA JACOBS

Making time

'The Lord who rescued me from the paw of the lion and the paw of the bear will rescue me from the hand of this Philistine.' (v. 37, NIV)

David had spent a lot of time with God while out in the fields alone with his sheep. The shepherd boy knows the Lord; we can see the depth of relationship he has with God in many of his psalms. David wasn't perfect, he got it wrong, but he was still a 'man after [God's] own heart' (Acts 13:22).

David trusts the Lord; he knows perfectly well that the God who has taken care of him in the past will take care of him now, as he faces the Philistine giant. He has seen the proof. God has delivered him before, so why should he stop now? That's confidence!

It's only when we really get to know someone, experience them coming through for us and the reliability of their friendship, that we can really begin to trust them. And that takes time. David didn't just turn up on the battlefield and declare he could fight the enemy and win. The odds seemed stacked against him; he was just a boy with a shepherd's sling. But David's trust wasn't in his own ability; he gave all the glory to God.

I came close to God when circumstances meant I couldn't live a 'normal' life due to illness and the resulting agoraphobia. I found he provided for me in ways I never expected, and he became very real to me. If we want to know true intimacy with God, to the point where he is our closest friend and ally, the one we rely on when all else fails, the main relationship in our lives, then we need to spend time nurturing that relationship with him, so that we might trust him. That means making time with him a priority.

How much time do you spend with Jesus during the week? Can you think about ways you can begin to spend more time with him, getting to know him more?

SHEILA JACOBS

Precious and loved

'Since you are precious and honoured in my sight… I love you… Do not be afraid, for I am with you.' (vv. 4–5, NIV)

To be known by God is a wonderful yet humbling thought. God calls us 'precious and honoured' (v. 4). In Psalm 139 we read that we are 'wonderfully made' (v. 14); we are known by God physically, emotionally and mentally. He knows how we are constructed. He understands our behaviour and why we act as we do. If we truly and fully grasped that we are understood by pure Love, then we might find ourselves feeling a lot less stressed when things seem to go wrong in our lives.

God is love – that's actually who he is (1 John 4:8). So, when we invite him into our lives, we are inviting Love to take over. Love can only act in one way – in our best interests. If we trust ourselves to Love, we need never be afraid. Psalm 91 tells us that we are rescued and protected because we know God. We are blessed.

Perhaps today you don't feel particularly blessed. Maybe you are living in fear. 1 John 4:18 tells us that 'perfect love drives out fear'. Why? Because fear is about being punished, about a bad outcome. If we trust ourselves to Love, then we step away from fear into confidence in the one who has said he will never leave or forsake us (Hebrews 13:5).

The more we get to know Jesus, the more time we spend with him, the more we will understand how much he loves us. We will be able to go to him with our deepest worries and anxieties, our joys and our desires. We love to be with people we love, don't we? As we deepen our relationship with our heavenly Father, then we will grow more in love with him and experience his presence more. And his presence, of course, is Love itself.

Slowly read aloud the verse above from the passage in Isaiah. Imagine Jesus saying this to you. Take your time. How will you respond?

SHEILA JACOBS

Forgiveness

When they had finished eating, Jesus said to Simon Peter, 'Simon son of John, do you love me more than these?' 'Yes, Lord,' he said, 'you know that I love you.' (v. 15, NIV)

Peter, James and John were the inner circle of Jesus' intimate companions. They ate with him, walked with him, talked with him, laughed and joked and had serious conversations with him. They knew him and yet, when his Lord was arrested, Peter had denied Jesus three times. Jesus had known this would happen and, after his resurrection, he singled out the errant disciple for a walk on the beach.

I wonder what Peter was thinking at this time. Perhaps he thought Jesus was going to tell him how disappointed he was in him, how he was disqualifying Peter from any further ministry: 'It's okay, we're still friends, I forgive you, but I don't trust you. So, we won't be as close as we were. You've blown it, Peter.' No! Reading the words of today's passage, a very different picture emerges.

Peter had denied Jesus three times, and three times Jesus asks Peter if he loves him. Twice, Jesus uses the word for the highest form of love, *agape*, God's love. Peter could hardly admit to loving Jesus that much; he had failed him. The third time, Jesus uses the word for friendship that Peter was comfortable with. He came down to Peter's level, and he is willing to come down to ours, even in a stable – a time we remember during the Advent season.

Peter is lovingly restored and given a new commission. He is to feed the Lord's flock, the mature ones and the little ones.

This is a story of forgiveness, and forgiveness is such an important part of intimacy. Unforgiveness in any relationship will surely sour it and create distance. God forgives us, as we forgive others. Unforgiveness will block our relationship with God. Is there anyone you need to forgive to clear the way for you to get close to Jesus?

Think about anyone you need to forgive. (Perhaps talk to a trusted Christian friend or leader if this is difficult for you.) If you can, bring that person to God now. Maybe you need to forgive yourself?

SHEILA JACOBS

Wandering off

'Therefore I am now going to allure her; I will lead her into the wilderness and speak tenderly to her'… 'In that day,' declares the Lord, 'you will call me "my husband"; you will no longer call me "my master".' (vv. 14, 16, NIV)

One of the greatest books in the Old Testament which expresses the love of God for his children – in this case the nation of Israel – is the book of Hosea. Hosea is asked by God to take an unfaithful wife and, after she has abandoned him, to take her back again. The Lord uses this whole event as a very powerful picture of his love and forgiveness for the people who so often walk away, go after other 'loves' and turn their back on him.

We too chase other gods or idols, other loves, and our own love for God can grow cold. In Hosea, God expresses the relationship between himself and his people as a marriage; he is their husband. In like manner, when we come to Christ, we enter an intimate relationship with someone who loves and feels and enjoys our company – and can be hurt when we turn from him.

It is often in the wilderness that we realise we have wandered far from our first love. In 1 Kings 19 we see how Elijah, after a great victory, finished up in the desert, feeling depressed and far from God. God gently restored him, spoke to him and ultimately gave him a new commission. When we find ourselves in wilderness situations, we can be sure that we are not alone. Sometimes it is God himself who leads us into these situations (Matthew 4:1), but so many times we wander off because we allow our relationship with Jesus to be placed on the backburner, replaced by other trinkets or worries.

We all have legitimate wilderness times, but let's not forget the one who speaks tenderly to us when all seems lost – calling us back to that intimacy he so desires.

If you feel you are in the wilderness, know that God is with you. Listen for his tender voice. You're not alone. He is drawing you close, even (and sometimes especially) during difficult times.

SHEILA JACOBS

Listening and doing

When the wine was gone, Jesus' mother said to him, 'They have no more wine.' 'Woman, why do you involve me?' Jesus replied. 'My hour has not yet come.' His mother said to the servants, 'Do whatever he tells you.' (vv. 3–5, NIV)

What a wonderful picture of intimacy this is! Mary knows her son is also the Son of God, the one whose father is not Joseph, but God himself. He is the Messiah. He is the very fullness of God in bodily form (Colossians 2:9). He is the human face of the divine presence.

Initially, Jesus seems reluctant to help. He knows who he is and what he has come to do. The timing will be perfect. Can you imagine the smile on his mother's face as she tells the servants to do whatever he says?

A great miracle occurs. Jesus turns the water into wine. Wine equates with joy in the Bible, so it's a picture of how he can bring joy into a barren situation.

How amazing it would be to know Jesus so well that we immediately obey when we feel his divine prompts. Doing whatever he tells us to do results in an exciting walk, and one that leads to further intimacy as we step out in faith.

To do what he tells us requires us to listen. Then, as we recognise the voice of the shepherd (John 10:3–4), we will know what he is saying to us. However, becoming familiar with his voice takes time and practice. Too often we mistake our own voice for his, and sometimes we hear voices from the past, perhaps condemning or accusing – words that cause us to doubt or fear or feel we aren't 'good enough'. We must remember we have an enemy who doesn't have our best interests at heart! Jesus comes to bring us into our destiny in him, while the enemy tries to scupper those plans. Let's make sure we are listening to the right voice and doing his will.

Lord, help me to hear your voice more clearly, so that I can do what you want me to do and be who you want me to be. I want to please you. Amen.

SHEILA JACOBS

Not disqualified!

Then, leaving her water jar, the woman went back to the town and said to the people, 'Come, see a man who told me everything I've ever done. Could this be the Messiah?' (vv. 28–29, NIV)

Last Sunday, we thought about hiding from God. Many things can persuade us to hide from him; maybe we feel shame or failure. These things can separate us from the intimacy of knowing him.

When Jesus spoke to the woman at the well, he was doing something a rabbi would never do – speaking to a woman who was unknown to him, alone and from a people-group who were deemed unacceptable – but he had important things to tell her. He was able to supply living water, the life of God, the new creation, as the Holy Spirit was poured out into her heart.

It is obvious that this woman lived a difficult life. She was avoiding company, collecting water at a time when other women would not be present, and she had a complicated backstory. Jesus told her that he knew all about it, yet he didn't judge her. There was no condemnation, just acceptance and the offer of new life, new hope, new ministry and new relationships.

Of all the people he could ever speak to, this woman had more reason than most to hide from him, but Jesus sought her out. Jesus seeks you out today, and me too.

There have been times when I have felt the weight of failure separate me from God. On one such occasion I 'saw' a picture of Jesus carrying a backpack full of heavy rocks. I noticed that I too was carrying a backpack. It was as if he said, 'Why are you carrying that? I am carrying it for you. The debt has been paid.' There's nothing stopping us from intimacy with Jesus – knowing him as we are fully known, loved and accepted.

Perhaps you feel disqualified from knowing God intimately. You're not!

Whatever your backstory, Jesus seeks you out. He won't condemn. He listens, restores and loves you. Is it time to hand everything over to him?

SHEILA JACOBS

Where I am

My Father's house has many rooms… And if I go and prepare a place for you, I will come back and take you to be with me that you also may be where I am. (vv. 2–3, NIV)

One evening, I felt God speaking to me about how much I meant to him. I was feeling low, and when I heard the Lord's quiet whisper, I listened intently. He told me that he had prepared a place for me, because he loved me so much that he wanted me to spend eternity with him; that he had given the best, his only Son, who had paid my debt of selfishness and separation from him; that I was free, and he wanted me to live in that freedom and enjoy his company. That was an intimate moment. I realised I was known by him, and that although at times I felt far from him, he was never far from me. I was his beloved daughter – precious, wanted and protected.

The lavish love of God is something we may struggle to receive, especially if we feel we have been let down by others. Why would God love me? Does he really care about me so much that he gave his only Son – for me? We can say the words, we know the scriptures, but can we personalise it? God is love, he is generous, he 'keeps no record' of our wrongs, in Christ (1 Corinthians 13:5). He wants us to be where he is. He longs for our company!

When I was very ill, I couldn't work or go to church. All I wanted to do was work for God, but I discovered in that season that he didn't want me to work for him, he wanted to do his work in and through me. There are many people who want to work for him, but I wonder how many of us want to sit quietly and just 'be' with him?

When we really love someone, just sitting in their presence, even in the same room, can be a delight. Thank God that he loves you and wants you to be in his presence!

SHEILA JACOBS

Remain in him!

Remain in me, as I also remain in you. No branch can bear fruit by itself; it must remain in the vine. Neither can you bear fruit unless you remain in me. (v. 4, NIV)

Speaking in the upper room to his disciples, before he faced arrest, trial and crucifixion, Jesus urges them to 'remain' in him. That, he says, is the way to bear fruit – good fruit, the evidence of a life transformed (Galatians 5:22–23). In the natural world, we know that fruit does not just happen. We pick apples because the apple tree has produced blossom, then fruit. Apples don't just appear on other trees; we don't get apples from a willow tree. In the same way, if we are connected to Jesus, his Spirit will produce fruit in us that is evidence of our connection, our root. We need to stay connected to Jesus if we want to bear good fruit – the fruit of who he is, his life in us through his Holy Spirit.

As we listen to his voice and choose his way for our lives, we will find ourselves becoming more and more like him. His life will 'leak out' of us, but the key to this transformation is in the connection. Once fruit is disconnected from the tree or the vine, it will begin the process of dying. We cannot afford to disconnect from Jesus! It's so easy to let other things steal our time from close communion with God – and consequently, we run the risk of trying to live the Christian life in our own strength.

I sometimes rearrange my schedule to be with close friends. We make it a priority to be present for people we care about, don't we? So, how much do we want to 'remain' in Jesus? Are we committed to spending time with him, getting to know his will and his way? If we do, our intimacy with God will surely bear good fruit!

Are you trying to live the Christian life in your own strength? Do you need to reconnect with Jesus? Remain in him!

SHEILA JACOBS

Stay close

When they saw the courage of Peter and John and realised that they were unschooled, ordinary men, they were astonished and they took note that these men had been with Jesus. (v. 13, NIV)

We are highly influenced by the people who are close to us, people we have chosen to be in our lives and with whom we share our joys and sorrows.

Peter and John were demonstrating lives lived with the one who had healed the sick and preached the good news of the kingdom of God. They were doing what Jesus had done. In Acts 3 we read of a lame man who was healed, leading to the disciples' heartfelt teaching – and jail time.

The eloquence of Peter's speech in Acts 4 does not read like the words of a simple fisherman. He was unschooled and ordinary. Where did the courage and authority to speak like this in front of learned men come from? The religious leaders of the day soon realised – 'these men had been with Jesus' (v. 13). They talked like him and they lived like him.

If we spend a lot of time with another person, we may start copying their words and idioms. Their beliefs may not mirror our own, but perhaps they make us think differently. Whoever we are intimate with begins to influence us.

The more time we spend with Jesus, the more we become like him. As we grow in intimacy with him, we begin to see the world – our family, people we know – in the same way as he sees them. We may find our attitudes begin to soften and change. Who he is begins to manifest in our lives.

I wonder, do people say of us, 'We can see that this person has been with Jesus'? Can they see Jesus in and through us, our words, our actions? Are they drawn to the person they see reflected in us?

Because we are so influenced by those with whom we spend the most time, imagine what it would be like if we spent more time in the presence of God!

SHEILA JACOBS

Discerning his presence

As they talked and discussed these things with each other, Jesus himself came up and walked along with them; but they were kept from recognising him. (vv. 15–16, NIV)

On the road to Emmaus, two distressed and disillusioned disciples are joined on the journey by a stranger. He turns out to be the resurrected Jesus, revealing himself through the scriptures and ultimately through the breaking of bread – a picture of what he has achieved for them and for us on the cross, when he died so that we need no longer be separated from God.

It's interesting that the disciples don't recognise Jesus at first, even though they must have known him well.

When I have been close to God, I've said, 'Lord, never let me be further away from you than I am right now.' Unfortunately, we do drift. Often, we slide away from intimacy with him, and we may feel a resultant sense of loss. It could be that we have walked with Jesus for quite a while and then things happen and we don't experience his presence as closely as we did. Sometimes Jesus *seems* to draw away from us. Why? It could be that we have displeased him or that he wants us to seek him more keenly or maybe he is just asking us to wait for him in the silence in quiet trust.

It might be that Jesus has been walking alongside us, yet we have never really known him, and are astonished when he reveals himself, inviting us to look for him more fully in his word.

It's important to add that sometimes our hearts can deceive us, and we need to always be aware that as our intimacy with God deepens, what we are learning should line up with the scriptures that speak of him.

Let's make every effort to not lose sight of him, even in times when heaven seems silent and we don't always discern his presence.

Lord, thank you that you are always walking with me, even though sometimes I don't feel your presence. Lord, help me to seek you and wait for you. Amen.

SHEILA JACOBS

Called child!

Because you are his sons, God sent the Spirit of his Son into our hearts, the Spirit who calls out, '*Abba*, Father.' So you are no longer a slave, but God's child; and since you are his child, God has made you also an heir. (vv. 6–7, NIV)

The Spirit of Jesus lives in us when we surrender our lives to him! We are no longer slaves to religious living, trying to attain right standing with God, but are called his child. It's a free gift for those who will accept it. We don't have to earn a place in a family! If we know Jesus, we are an adopted child of God. We belong. Indeed, we are a co-heir with Jesus (Romans 8:17). This is our identity. This is who we are.

Our experience with our own father may not have been a positive one, and we can often view God through that filter. If our father was absent, disinterested or harsh, we may picture our heavenly Father in such a way too. Indeed, we may find ourselves struggling with the idea of the lavish love of Father God, so we shy away from intimate companionship with him. We can end up living our Christian life at a distance from the source of it and consequently find it hard to see ourselves as a 'child' because we just don't know God as a loving Father.

Living the God-life was never meant to be religious striving, lived out in our own strength. It's meant to be an intimate connection, as God divinely downloads his own life into us.

When we wander – or run – away from the place of intimacy with God (or perhaps have never truly found it), we may find ourselves in a dry and lonely place. Let's remember that we need only go to our Father to know restoration, love and forgiveness. We come empty-handed to find his unconditional embrace.

In the place of intimacy with God, we discover a depth of love that outweighs every other love we have ever known or could know.

Find a quiet place and meditate on the verses above. What stands out for you? Perhaps today is the day to rediscover – or find – that intimacy with the one who calls you 'child'.

SHEILA JACOBS

So much closer

Let him lead me to the banquet hall, and let his banner over me be love… Catch for us the foxes, the little foxes that ruin the vineyards, our vineyards that are in bloom. (vv. 4, 15, NIV)

Song of Songs is about intimate love, a lover and his beloved. Jesus is our divine lover, and we, his people, the beloved. We need to always remember that his 'banner over [us]' is love (v. 4); that all we entrust to him will be worked out in love. It can't be otherwise; love is who he is (1 John 4:8). However, we must be aware of the 'little foxes' who can ruin a vineyard. We must be protective over our relationship with God and not allow any 'little foxes' to ruin our walk with him.

What are the 'little foxes' that might cause your intimacy with God to falter: fear, a sense of not being good enough, of wanting something (or someone) more than God's presence, of knowing there is something he wants you to put right in your life?

Today, we are as close to him as we want to be. Why do we stand far off when we could be so much closer? In Revelation 3:20 we read of Jesus standing at the door and knocking. Anyone who opens the door to him will find he steps into their life and will 'eat' with them. Sharing a meal usually shows that we really want to spend time with someone and enjoy their company. The thought of sharing a banquet with Jesus is just amazing, isn't it? If his banner over us is love, then surely we will want to open the door to that love?

As we reach the end of these notes about intimacy with God, let's put aside anything that may stop us, and step into new intimacy with him. Let's surrender fully to the grace and love of God and see what happens next!

Jesus, your banner over me is love! I want to throw the door open and invite you into my life afresh today. I don't want anything to stop that intimacy growing between us. Thank you! Amen.

SHEILA JACOBS

Asking questions of the Christmas story

Michele D. Morrison writes:

In a world seemingly dominated with bad news, it is so good to celebrate good news. Sometimes, though, even great news, as it becomes familiar, loses some of its initial pizzaz. So, it's good to shake up the way we hear and share good news, especially *the good news*, to remove the ho-hum and restore the wow.

Over the next fortnight, we are going to examine the Christmas story through the eyes of an investigative journalist, asking the questions: Who? What? When? Where? How? Why?

We are going to question if it matters that the Son of God was born into the world and didn't just appear. God appears several times in physical form in the Old Testament: to confirm a promise, to commission a specific task, to confide, to inspire, to save. God has interacted with humanity right from the beginning; we were created for relationship, and, heartbroken, he has sought us ever since we fell from grace in the garden.

In the awesome, sacrificial miracle of the incarnation, the Trinity chose to become one of us here on earth. In an act of supreme love, the triune God chose to separate, and the word of creation became flesh to dwell among us. The fact that God chose to father a child with Mary and be born both fully human and fully divine rooted that child, the Son of God, in history and changed his own perspective and appearance forever. The cross and resurrection released the Holy Spirit to inhabit the lives of believers and empower them to live the life of love to which God calls us all. What incredible sacrifice and revelation of God's love for his creation and creatures! God has always been fully committed.

Matthew opens his gospel with a genealogy, tracing Jesus' ancestral lineage. Mark opens his with a prophet's vision, placing Jesus both historically and prophetically. Luke goes into the practical detail of Jesus' conception and birth, and John gives us the spiritual DNA of Jesus. Each gospel writer is eager that believers in the future will know exactly who Jesus is.

Preparing these notes has been both a challenge and a joy, setting my heart on fire again for Jesus, my Saviour. So, get out your reporters' notebook, and let's ask the questions, reigniting our passion for the love who came down at Christmas.

From everlasting

In the beginning was the Word, and the Word was with God, and the Word was God. He was with God in the beginning. Through him all things were made. (vv. 1–3, NIV)

Who is this baby born in a manger, son of a young peasant girl from Nazareth? Does it really matter that Jesus was alive as the creator God before he was born into the world, fully human, fully divine? Does it matter that he is God incarnate, rather than a good human being whom God blessed with supernatural abilities and wisdom?

Genesis 3:15 foretells that Eve's offspring will crush the evil one. Even in the early days of creation, God foresaw Immanuel, Jesus: God with us.

In a sense the Old Testament chronicles the real gestation period of Jesus, Son of Man. The Lord appears at various times, from a different dimension, for a particular reason, and then he leaves. Humanity might aspire to obey his commands, but without the role model of Jesus – the perfect hybrid of God and human – and without the Holy Spirit who the risen Lord sends to indwell believers, our aspirations are hopeless.

It matters profoundly that Jesus is the Word, the creator from the beginning, who became flesh and made his dwelling among us.

As we consider the sacrifice he made, giving up his place in heaven to become a vulnerable human who was rejected, taunted, tortured and murdered, the unconditional love he has for his creation is life-changing. We can't fully appreciate who the baby in the manger is until we recognise that he is the Word made flesh who came to dwell among us, to impart the light of life and the power of the Spirit to enable us to live life to the full.

As a baby in Bethlehem, Jesus could do nothing and depended totally on his human parents. As human beings, we can do nothing and depend totally on Jesus.

Consider: The baby we worship at Christmas is older than time itself and yet part of the new creation. Pray: Your sacrifice, Jesus, is eternal. I surrender all to you, my God and my King. Amen.

MICHELE D. MORRISON

Prince of Peace

This means that God is transforming each one of you into *the Holy of Holies*, **his dwelling place, through the power of the Holy Spirit living in you! (v. 22, TPT)**

We ask again, who is Jesus? Could he be just another baby human who is later consecrated because he lived a saintly life, or is it critical that Jesus, the fully human baby, is fully God?

Yesterday, we saw that the heel of the baby born in the manger would crush Satan's head – only Jesus could defeat Satan. Today, we consider the enmity between God's chosen people and the Gentiles, remembering the words of John 3:16: 'For God so loved the world that he gave his one and only Son, that whoever believes in him shall not perish but have eternal life' (NIV). God's plan is to redeem the whole world, but enmity runs deep. We need the Prince of Peace.

Paul tells us that through Jesus' crucifixion, Jews and Gentiles have become one people. Jesus has broken down the wall of hostility that used to separate us and together, as one body, we are reconciled to God because of Jesus' sacrifice. The mission of the baby in the manger is restoration, redemption and peace – with God and with one another.

A certain medical diagnosis has highlighted my need to strengthen my core. This, I find, requires dogged tenacity in remembering to do frequent exercises. Building faith requires tenacity in surrendering to God. The core of our faith is strengthened as we let go of our pride and independence and surrender fully to God's love. His love destroys the barriers that are built through prejudice and unites us as one body in Christ. Two have now become one, and that is because Jesus is who he is – the eternal creator God.

Prince of Peace, who was with the Father from the beginning, help us to surrender the pride that keeps us in thrall to our own prejudices. Fill us now with your Spirit, Jesus, our Saviour. Amen.

MICHELE D. MORRISON

The family tree

'For the time is coming,' says the Lord, 'when I will raise up a righteous descendant from King David's line. He will be a King who rules with wisdom. He will do what is just and right.' (Jeremiah 23:5, NLT)

I am currently collating the genealogical information other family members have gathered about my ancestors and seeking to fill in the gaps. I come from 19th-century immigrants to the USA, and our recorded history starts in Europe. I am hoping to make a short trip to Germany to seek out my father's grandfather's family.

How important is genealogy? Is it just a first-world vanity, where many people hope to discover they are descended from royalty or someone famous, or is it important to know where you come from?

The Jewish people put great store in genealogies. The genealogy of Jesus is included in both the gospels of Matthew and of Luke. They differ in that Matthew presents the information in the traditional Jewish fashion, from Abraham forward, while Luke begins with Jesus and goes backwards. They also differ in who they include, and scholars can't agree on the reason for that. Interestingly, Matthew includes four women in his list: not women of stature but Gentile women, some associated with scandal. Jesus' human pedigree includes everyone.

The Jews knew that their Messiah would come from the line of David. Both Matthew and Luke link Jesus to David, which sets him in a royal line. Equally, both acknowledge Mary as Jesus' mother and Joseph as husband of Mary, known as the father of Jesus (Matthew 1:16; Luke 3:23).

When we ask, 'Who is Jesus?', his family tree gives us some answers. We are drawn back into the Old Testament, where we see the coherence of scripture and other indications that Jesus was not only foretold from the beginning but also in the beginning.

The infant Jesus is not just another infant. He is the son of a virgin, and he carries the genes of his Father God.

Sit quietly with a scrap of paper and a pen and jot down what difference it makes to you that Jesus is with us and that his lineage is remarkable on a human as well as divine level.

MICHELE D. MORRISON

Joy to the world!

The angel answered, 'The Holy Spirit will come on you, and the power of the Most High will overshadow you. So the holy one to be born will be called the Son of God.' (v. 35, NIV)

As the angel Gabriel reassured Mary that nothing was impossible for God, her response was one of enthusiastic assent: 'Yes! I will be a mother for the Lord!' A young teenage virgin, Mary could have had no idea of all the repercussions of her decision – but she'd have been acutely aware of some. Even claiming to have had an angelic visitation would have raised eyebrows, but to then also explain Gabriel's message would have seemed ludicrous, impossible even! Yet she believed it would happen to her just as the angel said. She trusted God.

We see here how important it was for Jesus to have Mary as his mother. A virgin, humble and devout, ready to submit to the Lord's plan. Divorce and stoning were two distinct possibilities, but Mary didn't look at the human outcome to the angel's message: she trusted God. 'May your word to me be fulfilled' (v. 38). Her situation was precarious; her reputation, even her life, were in danger. This was a situation fraught with difficulties.

And yet, when Elizabeth's unborn John heard Mary's voice, he danced with joy. Jesus is the good news. He sets our feet dancing. Whatever troubles we face, whatever situations we fear, whatever sorrows we grieve, Jesus sets our feet dancing when we focus on him.

Who is Jesus? The son of the virgin Mary, yes, and the Son of God, born of some mysterious union with the Spirit. All things are possible.

What impossible situation are you facing? What challenge has God set you which intimidates you? Let Mary be your role model. Look into the face of the Lord Jesus, breathe deep, and declare: 'May it be to me as you will.' Joy will be yours.

Lord Jesus, I thank you that you equip me for the tasks to which you call me. May I trust in your divine wisdom, your supernatural equipping and lean not on my own understanding. Amen.

MICHELE D. MORRISON

An inspiring role model

Watch for this – a virgin will get pregnant and bear a son; They will name him Immanuel (Hebrew for 'God is with us'). Then Joseph woke up. He did exactly what God's angel commanded. (vv. 23–24, MSG)

With our journalist's notebook filling up, we ask one last time: 'Who is Jesus?' Scripture identifies him clearly as the one foretold by Isaiah (7:14): the angel identified him clearly to Joseph in his restless dream.

These days, increasing numbers of people live in blended families. Joseph is a brilliant role model of a great stepfather. In a patriarchal culture, it would have been hugely challenging to play second fiddle to his (disgraced) wife, but Joseph obeys God as directed by the angel. Even before his dream, we see what kind of a man Joseph is. *The Message* describes him as 'chagrined but noble, determined to take care of things quietly so Mary would not be disgraced' (v. 19). How the heavenly Father's heart must have swelled with love for Joseph, seeing his humility and obedience – the same unquestioning obedience Mary shows. The perfect couple to raise Immanuel.

I wonder at what point the infant Jesus became conscious of his uniqueness. Scripture is silent on that until he turns twelve and lingers in the temple, clearly aware who his real Father is. How was this revealed to him? Presumably most powerfully by the Holy Spirit dwelling in him, but the teaching must have started on Mary's knee and at Joseph's workbench. Children love hearing stories of their birth and early years. What amazing stories Jesus would have heard, of angels singing, of shepherds bowing, of kings bringing gifts and of an evil king seeking his life and forcing them to flee.

Joseph taught Jesus his trade; side by side at the bench, hour by hour, they would have talked. Who was Jesus? The stepson of Joseph, an inspiring role model.

Lord Jesus, thank you for Joseph and Mary. Thank you for their humble willingness to obey, even in startlingly surprising and challenging circumstances. May I learn from their examples. Amen.

MICHELE D. MORRISON

Born in Bethlehem

'But you, Bethlehem Ephrathah, though you are small among the clans of Judah, out of you will come for me one who will be ruler over Israel.' (v. 2, NIV)

Does it matter where Jesus was born? The Messiah was prophesied to come from the house and lineage of David, and Bethlehem was known as the city of David, as Samuel had found him and anointed him king there.

Mary and Joseph knew each other in Nazareth. They were betrothed in Nazareth, but Nazareth was not the place where the Messiah should be born. Remember the words of Nathanael (John 1:46): Can anything good come from Nazareth?

The Jewish people knew that their Messiah was to come from the house of David. Mary and Joseph were both from David's line but had there not been a census at the time Jesus was due, that fact might have been obscured. The Father did everything to reveal the scriptural legitimacy of Jesus' claim. He co-ordinated it that a secular ruler, Augustus, eager to swell the coffers of Rome through taxation, declared a census must be taken in such a way, at that time.

Bethlehem means 'house of bread' – fertile fields yielded good crops. Bethlehem was also the source of sacrificial lambs for the temple in nearby Jerusalem. It was therefore a fitting birthplace for the Lamb of God. Other significant figures are associated with Bethlehem: Rachel was buried there; Ruth and Naomi returned there from Moab, to be drawn into the lineage that would produce David.

God is not a prisoner of circumstances. With him, all things are possible. Wherever you are living, whatever you are doing, if God has a plan that needs to take place somewhere else, he will move you. There is no need to agitate, to be anxious or to go to extraordinary lengths to engineer something. Trust in God. He will place you where you need to be, at the perfect moment.

Father God, thank you for putting Mary and Joseph in the right place, at the right time. Help me to trust you to put me in the right place, at the right time. I am so grateful for your grace and patience with me. Amen.

MICHELE D. MORRISON

The master orchestrator

Once when Zechariah's division was on duty and he was serving as priest before God, he was chosen by lot… And when the time for the burning of incense came, all the assembled worshippers were praying outside. (vv. 8–10, NIV)

At Christmas, we hear the stories of two miraculous births. They are often told in a way which highlights the apparent randomness of events and circumstances which all came together into the grandeur and majesty of the greatest symphony of all time: the symphony of salvation. We're going to look now at the timing of Jesus' birth, beginning with the individual stories which start soft and swell to a great crescendo as they mingle and entwine in harmony and counterpoint, as directed by the Father of all.

Can you imagine the smile on the face of the Father as he directs this great symphony? There is nothing random in God's timing: God can use rotas and choices by lot to bring about his purposes. I love the detail that Gabriel appears to Zechariah when all the worshippers are praying. Even in this, the greatest story ever told, God involves his people. Don't ever overlook the power of prayer.

There is such richness of love shown in the pregnancy stories of cousins Elizabeth and Mary. How tender is the Father to encourage young Mary's faith in her encounter with her much older cousin. This timing is perfect, and it is critical to the outworking of the story of redemption. The 'when' is important.

It could be that our historical timing of celebration may be askew, but that does not matter. Some scholars, considering the records of John the Baptist's conception in relation to Jesus' conception and bearing in mind that sheep would not have been in the fields in the deep winter, believe Jesus was probably conceived in December and born in September. John's gospel opens with the news that Jesus came to earth to tabernacle with us – a hint that he was born during the Feast of Tabernacles in autumn.

Whichever calendar date we choose to mark our celebration, that 'when' doesn't matter, but the original timing, set by the Father, is critical, and it is perfect.

MICHELE D. MORRISON

History is his story

But when the set time had fully come, God sent his Son, born of a woman, born under the law, to redeem those under the law, that we might receive adoption to sonship. (vv. 4–5, NIV)

In terms of world history, does it matter when the Son of God was born? Absolutely. Roman rule over the known western world linked the empire by a network of roads and routes which ultimately served to spread the gospel. The brutal persecution the Romans initiated against followers of Jesus resulted in many disciples travelling the highways and byways in all directions, taking the good news of Jesus to India, Africa and Europe. They could communicate the gospel through the lingua franca (Greek), then Latin: a gospel which brought hope, light and life into the hearts of those downtrodden and despairing.

The first to die because of the gospel was Jesus himself, cruelly executed on a cross, which fulfilled the prophecy of being hung on a tree, a curse and the Roman's preferred method of death for the worst of criminals. The cross would become a symbol of faith for millennia of believers. Details. God is intimately involved in every aspect of life, every detail. He cares about the small things (Zechariah 4:10).

Eastern religions sometimes refer to having all the stars aligned. God orchestrated the entrance of his much-loved Son, born in a troubled time, into a nation under the boot of cruel oppressors, into a poor family from an obscure village, in the time of Herod and Augustus: all the stars aligned to set the stage for our salvation story.

If you are weary from trying circumstances, disappointment, heartbreak or sorrow, the Lord hears the cry of your heart. He will act at the right moment, when all the details are perfectly aligned. Cast your burdens on the Lord because he cares for you.

Lord, may I be open to glimpse your hand in the most unlikely situation, at the most unexpected time. Raise my perspective, Lord, to align with yours. Amen.

MICHELE D. MORRISON

Human, yet divine

'Isn't this the carpenter's son? Isn't his mother's name Mary, and aren't his brothers James, Joseph, Simon and Judas? Aren't all his sisters with us?' (vv. 55–56, NIV)

Does it matter that Jesus was born into a working-class family, where he learned a trade and had siblings? Yes. It is essential.

The Bible tells us: 'For we do not have a high priest who is unable to feel sympathy for our weaknesses, but we have one who has been tempted in every way, just as we are – yet he did not sin' (Hebrews 4:15). For Jesus to identify with us and for us to identify with him, he had to be like us – just as vulnerable, just as tempted. He had to be a normal human being, who grew up in a hard-working family where he toiled alongside his dad. He had to be incontrovertibly human. Yet he remained sinless. How?

Jesus nurtured his relationship with the Father through his prayer life, through his knowledge of scripture and through his anointing with the Holy Spirit. When he was under pressure, tempted by the devil in the wilderness (Matthew 4:1–11), Jesus didn't rely on human wisdom to defeat the enemy. Instead, he quoted knock-out verses from scripture.

Jesus' Nazarene neighbours missed the point: instead of honestly asking how a local boy could be so wise, their attitude was one of 'hostile indifference' (v. 58, MSG). Yet he was inviting them to look at his beginnings, open their hearts to his teaching and understand that the kingdom of heaven was near and was open to all.

Jesus modelled how to live life to the full. If we follow his example by reading our Bibles, trusting in God and relying on the Holy Spirit, 'the right words will be there; the Spirit of your Father will supply the words' (Matthew 10:19–20 MSG).

We have a great high priest with whom we can identify. It started with a baby in a manger. The incarnation is critical.

Lord Jesus, may I bring to you all my questions, openly and honestly seeking to learn from you, knowing that because of the incarnation, you understand. Amen.

MICHELE D. MORRISON

Announced by angels

And there were shepherds living out in the fields near by, keeping watch over their flocks at night. An angel of the Lord appeared to them, and the glory of the Lord shone around them. (v. 8, NIV)

Does it matter how Jesus was born? The first humans to receive news of God's plan of redemption were Mary and Joseph. Another amazing angelic announcement is recorded here, where shepherds were blessed by the startling appearance of an angel giving them incredible news, followed by an awesome display of angelic glory and praise.

It may be that these were not ordinary shepherds but priests keeping watch over lambs who would be offered as sacrifices in the temple. The Mishnah (a record of Jewish oral tradition) recalls a custom from Pharisaic times which declared that all sheep must be reared in wilderness areas, except those destined for temple sacrifice. Bethlehem was not the wilderness. These shepherds, then, may have been watching over flocks destined for sacrifice, very aware of prophetic expectations of the perfect lamb, the Messiah, who would take away the sins of the world.

A more traditional understanding, though, is that the Son of God first revealed himself to the lowest of the low – dirty shepherds – because he came to redeem everyone, even those on the margins of life. Either way, when Jesus was born, the dark fields around Bethlehem were suddenly illuminated by the heavenly host singing their hearts out to God. John writes that the light had come into the world, but the darkness did not understand it. This was not a birth that went unnoticed. Baby Jesus was welcomed by the heavenly host, as well as the humble poor. He came for us all.

Lord, may your light burn brightly in me, driving out the darkness and lighting the way for others to meet with you. Amen.

MICHELE D. MORRISON

Born in a manger

**Mary went into labour, and there she gave birth to her firstborn son…
Mary and Joseph laid him in a feeding trough since there was no
available space in any upper room in the village. (Luke 2:6–7, TPT)**

What were the circumstances of Jesus' birth? Does it matter whether he
was born in his parents' house in Nazareth, in a palace in Jerusalem or in a
ground-floor public space of a relative's home in Bethlehem?

　We've spent years humming 'No room in the inn', a catchy tune sung
by all four of our children in their various nativity plays at the local school.
However, according to Middle Eastern experts and The Passion Translation, Jesus' parents would not have been going from one motel to the next
and encountering 'No vacancy' signs. As direct descendants of David, it is
likely they would have had relatives in the town and so they would have
gone to stay with family members. Trouble was, everyone else was there
to register, and all the upper rooms traditionally reserved for guests were
full, so they sheltered in an overflow – the ground-floor, all-purpose room
which housed feeble animals overnight. This wasn't a stable, but it would
have had a drinking trough and manger cut into the bedrock.

　It might not be so different from a stable as in an inn, but given they
would have taken refuge with relatives, they wouldn't have been ignored.
There must have been witnesses to the birth, kindly women helping Mary,
family members who were surprised by the string of shepherds guided
there by an angelic host.

　Nothing about Jesus' birth was private or secret. Right from the beginning, the circumstances of his life were displayed for the world to see.
There were witnesses who could corroborate the claim that Immanuel was
born of Mary. He was a helpless baby who, astonishingly, was also God.

---

*The humble nature of Jesus' birth meant that he experienced all the depriva-
tions and insecurities of those who live in poverty, whose lives are threatened
and whose worth is questioned. What a Saviour!*

MICHELE D. MORRISON

Jesus' mission statement

'The Spirit of the Lord is upon me, and he has anointed me to be hope
for the poor, healing for the brokenhearted, and new eyes for the blind,
and to preach to prisoners, "You are set free!"' (v. 18, TPT)

We have been asking ourselves many questions as we have studied the
accounts of Jesus' birth, and now we come to perhaps the most important one: why? Throughout the Old Testament, the coming of a saviour is
prophesied – one who will save his people, bringing hope and restoration.
Here, we see Jesus in his home synagogue, reading familiar words from
Isaiah and identifying himself as the anointed one sent to redeem the poor,
brokenhearted, blind and imprisoned. This is Jesus' mission statement.
He came to bring hope and healing and to teach us how to live different.

Last night, we had a barbecue. There were seven of us gathered around
a table in the garden – five Christians and two non-believers, one of them
a Ukrainian refugee who has never encountered the gospel. Conversation
ranged over many topics, but the consistent theme was a sigh of despair at
the state of the world. We live in a weary world, and I awoke this morning
convicted that I did not express the reason for my hope that we are not
doomed. I have written an email to everyone, rather belatedly expressing
my faith in the Lord who loves us and who took on human form in order to
set us free from the law of sin and death.

It can be daunting to speak words of hope as we're nodding in agreement with words of despair, but our hope is in the one who came at Christmas, Immanuel, God with us, the light of lights.

Jesus needed the anointing of the Spirit to fulfil his calling. How much
more, then, do we need the Holy Spirit's enabling in our lives?

Lord Jesus, anoint and inspire me today, that I might be your mouthpiece,
speaking words that bring hope to the weary, fill heavy hearts with joy and
point people back to you. Amen.

MICHELE D. MORRISON

Bridging the gap

The Son is the image of the invisible God, the firstborn over all creation. (v. 15, NIV)

Why did God need to take on human form?

For centuries, God's mighty acts of power on his people's behalf revealed his forgiving love for his children, but time after time his people turned their backs on him. The Father's essence was beyond their power to comprehend and impossible to relate to or obey. As this passage notes, we humans were alienated from God, our bad behaviour making us his enemies.

What was needed was someone to bridge the gap between heaven and earth, someone with whom humanity could identify, relate and respond. Someone through whom we could be reconciled to the Father.

In Jesus, the transcendent God became immanent. The Bible is clear on this point: when we see Jesus, we see the Father. 'The Son is the radiance of God's glory and the exact representation of his being, sustaining all things by his powerful word' (Hebrews 1:3).

'The radiance of God's glory' contained in the human body of Jesus of Nazareth. Wow! Philip demanded, 'Show us the Father.' How frustrated Jesus must have been! 'Anyone who has seen me has seen the Father,' he responded. 'Don't you know me?' (John 14:8–10).

Jesus invites us into an intimate relationship with the triune God. The book of Revelation says that Jesus stands at the door of each of our hearts and knocks (3:20). When we respond positively, inviting him in, he steps inside and becomes the most trustworthy of friends, eager to guide us into life in all its fullness.

By allowing himself to be 'found in appearance as a man' (Philippians 2:8), Jesus became our brother, affirming humans as children of God, with all the dignity and value that position confers.

'Don't you believe that I am in the Father, and that the Father is in me?' (John 14:10).

It is a breathtaking thought that God loved us so much that he was willing to bridge the huge distance between himself and humans by a supreme act of sacrificial grace.

MICHELE D. MORRISON

price

> ...ed for our transgressions, he was crushed for our
> ...; the punishment that brought us peace was on him, and by
> ...unds we are healed. (v. 5, NIV)

One last time, we consider why Jesus was born. This chapter in Isaiah fore-tells his coming. He was born to be the Saviour of the world: to free us from our sins and to rescue us from the tyranny of death. Here, Isaiah describes the level of suffering Jesus endured in order to save us.

Sin has a high price tag: death. Jesus paid that price. He is the Lamb of God who takes away our sins (John 1:29). Through him, and him alone, we are saved.

When I was a little girl, grocery stores gave out redemption stamps calculated according to the amount a shopper spent. My mother carefully stuck these stamps into books, to be traded in for some commodity she needed. She earned the 'gift' because of the money she spent. Sometimes Christians act as if our good deeds are stamps in a heavenly redemption scheme, as if we must earn our ticket to heaven. But we can do nothing by ourselves; it by faith we are saved (Ephesians 2:5).

When we were still dead in our sins, Jesus died for us. He doesn't wait for us to prove ourselves worthy, because that is impossible. None of us is worthy.

His blood cleanses us from all our sins, so that the Holy Spirit can live within us and enable us to be changed forever, to be made holy. Our sins died with him on the cross, and we rise in him because of his righteous-ness. His resurrection put paid to death.

The good news of the Christmas story is that love came down and dwelt among us and changed everything, forever.

Joy to the world! The Lord has come! Spend some time praising God for the gift of his Son and all that he has done for us.

MICHELE D. MORRISON

Psalm 19: two hymns and a prayer

Jackie Harris writes:

We've spent some time studying the Christmas story and thinking about God's revelation through Jesus – what the details of the story tell us about God and his purposes. In these last three days of the year, we are going to consider two other ways God has revealed himself to humankind.

Our text is Psalm 19, which contains many well-known verses. The opening line – 'The heavens declare the glory of God' (v. 1, NIV) – has been the inspiration for countless hymns and worship songs, while the closing prayer – 'May these words of my mouth and this meditation of my heart be pleasing in your sight, Lord, my Rock and my Redeemer' (v. 14, NIV) – used to be the basis for the standard prayer from the pulpit before the sermon was given. Perhaps it still is in many churches.

The psalm divides beautifully into three parts. It is attributed to King David and thought to be a composite of two originally separate hymns – a hymn of creation (vv. 1–6) and a hymn celebrating God's instruction and teaching (vv. 7–10) – and a prayer. The three parts fit together as a response to the revelation of God.

Not only does the psalm divide into three sections, but each section features a different name for God. In verses 1–6, the word used is *El*, the most generic name for God in the original Hebrew. These verses describe God's revelation of himself through his created world. The heavens reveal God's glory and majesty to everyone throughout the world.

In verses 7–9, God is referred to as *Yahweh*, meaning 'the Lord'. In these verses David celebrates God's revelation to his chosen people through his laws and teaching. God's word reveals his moral character and instructs his people how to be right with him so they can flourish.

The latter part of the psalm is David's response, and here David calls God his rock and redeemer. These are more personal names, arising from David's experience of God and recognition that God is his protector and rescuer.

As we read through this psalm of praise and prayer, let's give thanks for God's revelation to us though his world and through his word and, like David, seek that close relationship and openness that enables us to know 'God with us' throughout the year ahead.

... the heavens

...eclare the glory of God; the skies proclaim the work of
...(v. 1, NIV)

W... ...asn't been awed by a beautiful sunrise or sunset, a starry night sky or a dramatic thunderstorm? Perhaps you've seen the spectacle of the northern lights, watched an eclipse or gazed at a blood moon. It's easy to see why the skies inspired David to praise.

In these first six verses, David reveals how God has spoken to us, revealing aspects of his character through his amazing creation. First, the majestic beauty of a sunrise and sunset reveals God's power and craftsmanship. I love the image of God pitching a tent for the sun (v. 4) and then the sun emerging as a bridegroom in full splendour as it rises in the eastern sky (v. 5). Second, the constant rising and setting of the sun reflects God's faithfulness and consistency. Third, we see something of God's kindness and generosity in creating something that everyone can see and experience. 'Their voice goes out into all the earth' (v. 4) and nothing is deprived of the sun's warmth (v. 6).

God reveals his glory to all humankind, and it is a powerful witness.

Paul develops this teaching in his letter to the Romans: 'For since the creation of the world God's invisible qualities – his eternal power and divine nature – have been clearly seen' (1:20). In other words, God has given us such amazing evidence of his power and glory that there is no excuse for humankind to ignore him or reject him.

If you can, spend some time outside today. Whether or not you can see and feel the sunshine, praise God for the wonder of the skies and his continuing care for all that he has made.

'When I consider your heavens, the work of your fingers, the moon and stars, which you have set in place, what is mankind that you are mindful of them... Lord, how majestic is your name in all the earth!' (Psalm 8:3–4, 9)

JACKIE HARRIS

The gift of God's word

**The statues of the Lord are trustworthy, making wise the simple…
They are more precious than gold… sweeter than honey.**
(vv. 7, 10, NIV)

How much do you value your Bible? I guess a lot of us will have more than one copy in our homes. I remember being very challenged when I heard about a community of Christians who shared one copy. The pastor separated the pages of this one, precious copy so that each person could have a portion of scripture to read. They would commit chunks of scripture to memory before passing on their pages and receiving a new section to read. Like David, they valued God's word as a precious gift.

These verses are a real encouragement to read and study our Bible every day. Look at the different words David uses for God's word: law and statutes (v. 7), precepts and commands (v. 8). These words imply authority. We need to give our full attention to what we read, because God's ways are good for us – 'They are sweeter than honey' (v. 10).

The previous verses outline why they are good for us. God's word is described as perfect, trustworthy, right and radiant. We can trust what God says. His word is constant and enlightening and tells us everything we need to know. When we turn to God's word, we will find wisdom, joy and insight and our souls will be refreshed and revived.

Knowing God's word and letting it inform, guide and change us enable us to live the way God wants us and designed us to live, which is the reward David speaks of in verse 11.

Let David's enthusiasm encourage you in your own Bible study – perhaps to persevere with some difficult passages, to memorise some verses or to spend more time studying the scriptures.

Thank God for the gift of his word. Pray for those who do not have easy access to the Bible and for those involved in translation or distribution work to make the scriptures more readily available.

JACKIE HARRIS

om sin

...den faults. Keep your servant also from wilful sins;
...t rule over me. Then I will be blameless, innocent of great
...ssion. (vv. 12–13, NIV)

Confession is not a popular subject. As an editor, I have struggled on a couple of occasions to find anyone willing to write on the topic – much nicer to put the focus on God's forgiveness and love than on our sin and shortcomings. David, however, has no such qualms. Having reflected on how God's world reveals his grandeur and how God's word instructs and nourishes us, his response is to consider his own failings and need of God's help and correction.

David recognises three types of sin: first, hidden sins (v. 12) – things he might be unaware of that need to be brought to light and dealt with; second, wilful sins (v. 13) – the things he is all too aware of that go against God's standards; and third, sins of word and thought (v. 14). David is aware that wrong thoughts lead to wrong words and actions, and so he asks God to make him mindful of what is going on in his heart.

David is prepared to face his sin and submit to God's probing because he knows he is loved by God. He has praised God for being an awesome creator and lawgiver, but here he comes before God who is his rock and redeemer – one who protects and rescues and offers rest.

God invites us to do the same. He has paid the price for our sin by sending his Son to die in our place. Therefore, we need not fear to let him search our hearts. We can confess our sin, knowing he will forgive us and 'purify us from all unrighteousness' (1 John 1:9).

On the eve of a new year, use David's prayer as the basis for your own confession, trusting that God wants to be for you a rock of refuge and your redeemer through all the days ahead.

JACKIE HARRIS

BRF Ministries

Inspiring people of all ages to grow in Christian faith

BRF Ministries is the
home of Anna Chaplaincy,
Living Faith, Messy Church
and Parenting for Faith

As a charity, our work would not be possible without
fundraising and gifts in wills.
To find out more and to donate,
visit brf.org.uk/give or call +44 (0)1235 462305

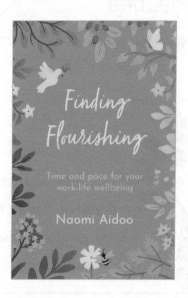

In our fast-paced world, *Finding Flourishing* redefines wellbeing as an accessible daily pursuit, even for the busiest among us. Naomi Aidoo presents a practical and tangible approach to achieving wellbeing, one that enhances your day-to-day mentally, emotionally and spiritually. This book is an interactive journey with thought-provoking questions, journal prompts, and the opportunity to reflect on daily life from a spiritual perspective, helping you discover a path to everyday wellbeing.

Finding Flourishing
Time and pace for your work–life wellbeing
Naomi Aidoo
978 1 80039 274 8 £8.99
brfonline.org.uk

To order

Online: **brfonline.org.uk**
Telephone: **+44 (0)1865 319700**
Mon–Fri 9.30–17.00

Delivery times within the U~~~
normally 15 working days. Prices are
correct at the time of going to press
but may change without prior notice.

Title	Price	Qty	Total
Day by Day with God (Sep–Dec 2024) – single copy	£4.99		
Day by Day with God (Jan–Apr 2025) – single copy	£4.99		
Finding Flourishing	£8.99		

POSTAGE AND PACKING CHARGES			
Order value	UK	Europe	Rest of world
Under £7.00	£2.00		
£7.00–£29.99	£3.00	Available on request	Available on request
£30.00 and over	FREE		

Total value of books	
Donation	
Postage and packing	
Total for this order	

Please complete in BLOCK CAPITALS

Title .... First name/initials .... Surname ....

Address ....

.... Postcode ....

Acc. No. .... Telephone ....

Email ....

Method of payment

❑ Cheque (made payable to BRF) ❑ MasterCard / Visa

Card no. ☐☐☐☐ ☐☐☐☐ ☐☐☐☐ ☐☐☐☐ ☐☐☐☐

Expires end ☐M☐M ☐Y☐Y Security code ☐☐☐   Last 3 digits on the reverse of the card

We will use your personal data to process this order.
From time to time we may send you information about
the work of BRF Ministries. Please contact us if you wish to discuss
your mailing preferences. Our privacy possible is available
at **brf.org.uk/privacy.**

Please return this form to:

BRF Ministries, 15 The Chambers, Vineyard, Abingdon OX14 3FE | **enquiries@brf.org.uk**

For terms and cancellation information, please visit **brfonline.org.uk/terms.**

Bible Reading Fellowship (BRF) is a charity (233280) and company limited by guarantee (301324), registered in England and Wales

...*ith God* is available from Christian bookshops
...y also be available through your church book agent or
... distributes Bible reading notes in your church.

...ou may obtain *Day by Day with God* on subscription direct from
... There are two kinds of subscription:

...dual subscription
covering 3 issues for 4 copies or less, payable in advance
(including postage & packing).

To order, please complete the details on page 144 and return with the appropriate payment to: BRF Ministries, 15 The Chambers, Vineyard, Abingdon OX14 3FE

You can also use the form on page 144 to order a gift subscription for a friend.

Group subscription
covering 3 issues for 5 copies or more, sent to one UK address (post free).

Please note that the annual billing period for group subscriptions runs from 1 May to 30 April.

To order, please complete the details on page 143 and return with the appropriate payment to: BRF Ministries, 15 The Chambers, Vineyard, Abingdon OX14 3FE

You will receive an invoice with the first issue of notes.

All our Bible reading notes can be ordered online by visiting
brfonline.org.uk/collections/subscriptions

All subscription enquiries should be directed to:
BRF Ministries, 15 The Chambers, Vineyard, Abingdon OX14 3FE
+44 (0)1865 319700 | **enquiries@brf.org.uk**

DBDWG0324

DAY BY DAY WITH GOD GROUP SUBSCRIPTION FORM

All our Bible reading notes can be ordered online by visiting
brfonline.org.uk/collections/subscriptions

The group subscription rate for *Day by Day with God* will be £14.97 per person until April 2025.

☐ I would like to take out a group subscription for .... (quantity) copies.

☐ Please start my order with the January 2025 / May 2025 / September 2025* issue. I would like to pay annually/receive an invoice* with each edition of the notes. (*delete as appropriate)

Please do not send any money with your order. Send your order to BRF Ministries and we will send you an invoice.

Name and address of the person organising the group subscription:

Title .... First name/initials .... Surname ....

Address...

.... Postcode ....

Telephone .... Email ....

Church..

Name and address of the person paying the invoice if the invoice needs to be sent directly to them:

Title .... First name/initials .... Surname ....

Address...

.... Postcode ....

Telephone .... Email ....

We will use your personal data to process this order. From time to time we may send you information about the work of BRF Ministries. Please contact us if you wish to discuss your mailing preferences. Our privacy policy is available at **brf.org.uk/privacy.**

Please return this form to:
BRF Ministries, 15 The Chambers, Vineyard, Abingdon OX14 3FE |
enquiries@brf.org.uk

For terms and cancellation information, please visit **brfonline.org.uk/terms**.

Bible Reading Fellowship is a charity (233280) and company limited by guarantee (301324), registered in England and Wales

To order online, please visit **brfonline.org.uk/collections/subscriptions**

☐ I would like to give a gift subscription (please provide both names and addresses)

☐ I would like to take out a subscription myself (complete your name and address details only once)

Title _____ First name/initials _____ Surname _____

Address _____

_____ Postcode _____

Telephone _____ Email _____

Gift subscription name _____

Gift subscription address _____

_____ Postcode _____

Gift subscription (20 words max. or include your own gift card):

_____

_____

Please send *Day by Day with God* beginning with the January 2025 / May 2025 / September 2025 issue (*delete as appropriate*):

(*please tick box*)	UK	Europe	Rest of world
1-year subscription	☐ £19.50	☐ £26.85	☐ £30.75
2-year subscription	☐ £38.40	N/A	N/A

Optional donation to support the work of BRF Ministries £ _____

Total enclosed £ _____ (cheques should be made payable to 'BRF')

Please charge my MasterCard / Visa with £ _____

Card no. ☐☐☐☐ ☐☐☐☐ ☐☐☐☐ ☐☐☐☐

Expires end ☐M☐M ☐Y☐Y Security code ☐☐☐ Last 3 digits on the reverse of the card

We will use your personal data to process this order. From time to time we may send you information about the work of BRF Ministries. Please contact us if you wish to discuss your mailing preferences. Our privacy policy is available at **brf.org.uk/privacy.**

Please return this form to:
BRF Ministries, 15 The Chambers, Vineyard, Abingdon OX14 3FE |
enquiries@brf.org.uk

For terms and cancellation information, please visit **brfonline.org.uk/terms.**

Bible Reading Fellowship is a charity (233280) and company limited by guarantee (301324), registered in England and Wales

DBDWG0324